HABITUDES®
FOR THE JOURNEY

IMAGES
THAT FORM
LEADERSHIP
HABITS &
ATTITUDES

THE ART OF NAVIGATING
TRANSITIONS

BY
DR TIM
ELMORE

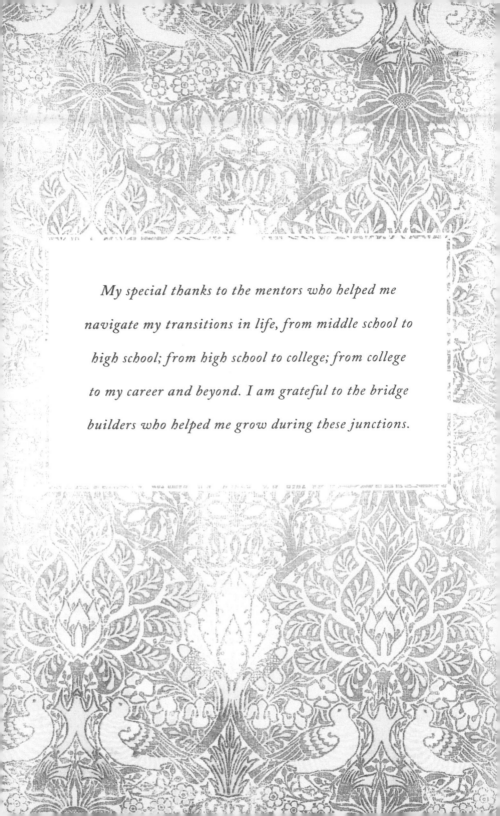

My special thanks to the mentors who helped me navigate my transitions in life, from middle school to high school; from high school to college; from college to my career and beyond. I am grateful to the bridge builders who helped me grow during these junctions.

Published in Atlanta, Georgia by Poet Gardner Publishers in association with "Growing Leaders, Inc." (www.GrowingLeaders.com)

ISBN: 978-0-9886201-0-0

Printed in the United States of America

Library of Congress Cataloguing-in-Publication Data

TABLE OF CONTENTS

BEFORE YOU READ ANYTHING ELSE...

It sounds cliché, but everyone must learn to navigate life's mountains (its greatest pleasures) and valleys (its toughest circumstances). Seasoned travelers get this. They know that some days the trip is easy and sometimes it's hard. They are not moved by either flattery or criticism. They can move fast and slow. It's all part of the territory. In this simple and brief volume, we'll look at your life as though it were a trip—using images to describe the realities you'll discover along the way.

The bottom line? To remind you how to successfully navigate the journey. You can win in the end. You can reach your desired destination despite the transitions you experience today.

Why do some not only finish school but finish well…while others fall short? What skills do we need to reach our highest potential? We've all asked these questions as we strive to achieve our personal best. Some have figured it out. Decoding the secrets of success is now a multi-billion-dollar industry. People go to seminars to learn them; parents pay large sums of money to give their kids the "success" advantage; leaders seek the newest tactics to gain any competitive edge.

Grit is the Secret

I believe one key is figuring out how to negotiate life's transitions. It almost always comes down to the junctions. The change points. The sharp turn on a trip; the handoff in a relay race; halftime at a football game. It's in these times we learn the power of "grit." Journalist Josh Linkner reminds us, "It turns out that good old-fashioned grit is the number one indicator of high performance." Grit can be defined as "perseverance and passion for long-term goals." Research reveals that grit, as a trait, has "better predictability for success than IQ."

The experts break it down and list these attributes as the building blocks of grit:

- A clear goal

- Determination despite others' doubts

- Self-confidence about figuring it out

- Humility about knowing it doesn't come easy

- Persistence despite fear

- Patience to handle the obstacles that obscure the path

- A code of ethics to live by

- Flexibility in the face of roadblocks

- A capacity for human connection and collaboration

- A recognition that accepting help does not equate to weakness

- A focus and appreciation of each step in the journey

- A loyalty that never sacrifices connections along the way

- An inner strength to help propel you to your goal

It's Inside of You...

Fortunately, grit is an inner quality we can all develop. There's no prerequisite. Nothing in our background or our situation has the power to take away our determination. We can push forward and take advantage of our potential and the opportunities around us.[1]

But it will all depend on how well you navigate your particular journey.

A WORD ABOUT IMAGES

We live in a culture rich with images. We grew up with photographs, TV, movies, videos, MTV, VH1 and DVDs. Many of us grew up watching YouTube. We can't escape the power of the visual image—and most of us don't want to.

I've learned over my career that most of us are visual learners. We like to see a picture, not just hear a word. Author Leonard Sweet says that images are the language of the 21st century, not words. Some of the best communicators in history taught using the power of the metaphor and image. One example is Martin Luther King Jr. and his "I Have a Dream" speech, during the Civil Rights movement. Tom Peters once wrote, "The best leaders . . . almost without exception and at every level, are master users of stories and symbols."

Why? Because pictures stick. We remember pictures long after words have left us. When we hear a speech, we often remember the stories from that speech, more than the phrases used by the speaker, because they painted a picture inside of us. Pictures communicate far more than mere words. In fact, words are helpful only as they conjure up a picture in our minds. Most of us think in pictures. If I say the word "elephant," you don't picture the letters: e-l-e-p-h-a-n-t. You picture a big gray animal. Pictures are what we file away in our minds. They enable us to store huge volumes of information. There's an old phrase that has stood the test of time: A picture is worth a thousand words. I believe it's true. I pursued a degree in both commercial art as well as theology in college. That's when I recognized the power of the image. Now I get to combine the power of teaching leadership principles with the power of pictures. I hope they linger in your mind and heart. I hope you discover layers of reality in them as you grow. I trust they'll impact you as profoundly as they have me.

The Journey

This book is just one of several *Habitudes*® books. Each is designed to furnish pictures you can discuss with a community of people. Each image represents a timeless, universal principle. Each picture contains layers of reality, and your discussion can go as deep as you allow it to go. This particular book will illumine your decisions as you move from one place in your life to another. You have probably already figured out that life is full of transitions—from middle school to high school; from high school to a college or a job; from college to career. Each transition is an opportunity to establish great habits, make great choices and meet great people…or an opportunity to absolutely fail at all of this. Some young people aren't able to navigate the changes in their lives, and they get off track. Eventually they find themselves at a destination they don't like because they didn't make the right moves at the crucial times. This discussion guide was designed to prevent that. In fact, my goal is to help you get to where you want to go.

Some sociologists describe this generation as EPIC: Experiential, Participatory, Image-driven and Connected. If that's true, I believe we'll get the most out of resources that give us an image, an experience and a way to connect with each other. Each of these books provides you not only with an image, but a handful of discussion questions, a self-assessment and an exercise in which you can participate. Dive in and experience each one of them. My hope is that they become signposts that guide you, warn you and inform you on your leadership journey.

Dr. Tim Elmore

Growing Leaders

[Windshields and Rearview Mirrors]

Windshields and Rearview Mirrors

EVERYONE FOCUSES ON SOMETHING—THE PAST OR THE FUTURE. WHERE DOES YOUR ENERGY COME FROM? WHEN OUR DREAMS ARE BIGGER THAN OUR MEMORIES, WE GAIN ENERGY FROM THE HOPE THAT LIES AHEAD. OFTEN, WE MUST LET GO OF THE COMFORT FROM OUR PAST TO MAKE PROGRESS.

When I was learning to drive, my dad noticed something strange about my newfound driving habits. After he taught me to check the rearview mirror before changing lanes—so I could see the cars around me—I got enamored with the whole process. I know it sounds strange, but as I drove, I kept looking in the rearview mirror. Over and over again. How cool was it to see what was right behind me (especially if it was a police car) without having to turn around! A simple peek could do it all. Well, I soon learned it was dangerous: I almost had a wreck. My dad had to shout, "Stop looking at all the cars behind you and focus on the road ahead of you!"

Note to self. That was good advice. I soon realized that rearview mirrors were good to glance at, but not to gaze at. Most of the time, it's best to look straight ahead.

I know two students who graduated from college last year, Shane and Evan. They both made good grades in school and were very active in clubs and intramural sports. I soon saw one big difference between them, however. Shane moved right into a job and began building his career. He was excited to meet the people on his new team and learn the ropes of his company. Evan didn't move forward quite as well. It wasn't that he couldn't find a job—he got one right away. It was that he never quite let go of his past. He continued going back to campus; he stayed focused on the events at his alma mater and was preoccupied with his classmates on Facebook. None of that is bad—but he never embraced his new role as an employee. His teammates at work could tell he wasn't really engaged. No matter what they did, Evan just wanted to stay in school, mentally.

I think Evan had the same problem I did with the rearview mirror. He should have been *glancing* at what was behind him—but *gazing* at what was ahead of him. Instead, he spent most of his time looking backward, which prevented him from moving forward.

In fact, you might say he almost had a wreck—his supervisor had to confront him and ask if he planned to stay long. He told Evan he wouldn't make it unless he buckled down and got serious about his work. Ouch.

This Habitude is not simply about letting go of the past. It is important to sustain friendships we've made along the way. We should be grateful for fun memories and good times. Our past will always help shape our future. But sometimes, the past can hold us back. If our memories are more important than our dreams—we are in trouble. If we prefer to look in the rearview mirror instead of the windshield, we'll get stuck—and maybe wreck. Holding on to the comfort of our past can keep us from grabbing the adventure that lies in our future.

Here's a question for you: Where does your energy come from—the past or the future?

Seriously. How would you answer that question? Some people become fearful about the future because of a single factor: They love the familiar and the comfortable. They only get energy from grasping what's behind them. Sadly, this confines them and even enslaves them, preventing them from seeing or seizing opportunities, new friendships, or new freedoms they might otherwise enjoy.

Years ago, a television report revealed how poachers caught monkeys in certain African countries. It was quite simple. They hollowed out a coconut, then made a hole in the surface just big enough for a monkey's hand. Next, they filled the coconut with jelly beans. Then they attached one end of a chain to the coconut, and the other end to a stake driven into the ground. The coconut was literally a ball and chain. It was a trap. As the monkeys sniffed the jelly beans and curiously visited the coconut, they were so enraptured by the candy that they didn't notice the chain or stake. Finally, one of them would reach into the coconut and grab a handful of the candy. At this point, one of the poachers came forward to throw a net around the monkey. Surprisingly, the primate could have run away free—but it never did. Why? It couldn't let go of the jelly beans. Freedom was available—but not achievable, because it imprisoned itself, holding on to the candy. Sound familiar?

A university once conducted a study on "peace of mind." Researchers sought the greatest factors that contributed to people's emotional and mental stability. The top five they discovered were:

1. Refusing to live in the past.

2. The absence of suspicion, resentment and regret.

3. Not wasting time and energy fighting conditions you cannot change.

4. Forcing yourself to get involved in the current world around you.

5. Refusing to indulge in self-pity.

Do you notice a pattern in their findings? All five of the factors above have to do with handling the *rearview mirror* and the *windshield* well.

Letting go of what's already happened and embracing what's in front of you. On your journey, can you peer out in front of you and become excited about the horizon? Can you gain more energy from the future than the past? Based on our qualitative research at Growing Leaders, the most common reasons students get "stuck in the past" are:

- They are victims of time. They can't seem to break free of old patterns.

- They are victims of relationships. They stay involved with people who hold them back.

- They are victims of comfort/nostalgia. They fear that their best days are in the past.

Try This Remedy

In response, we recommend the following simple new habits and attitudes:

1. Replace comfort with curiosity.
   Choose to leave the comfortable to pursue the compelling.
   Hunt for new horizons to conquer.

2. Reject being a victim of your circumstances.
   Don't let anyone control your emotions or your response to life.
   It is your life, after all.

3. Renew your commitment to embrace opportunities.
   Hang out with different people. Search for new challenges that will stretch you.

4. Relinquish the past and create new memories.
   Perhaps it's time to let go of the old trophies and ribbons and go earn some new ones.

Almost every culture celebrates each new year. In ancient Rome, the god Janus was a key symbol. (Our month of January is named after him.) Interestingly, he had two heads—one to look forward and the other to look backward. You might say the Romans recognized the value of the rearview mirror and the windshield. Later, an Italian custom was born. At the stroke of midnight on New Year's Eve, people began tossing possessions into the streets—anything that held a negative memory or connotation. They simply got rid of it and started anew. In doing this, they declared "Out with the old; let's start fresh." Not a bad custom as a new year begins.

After speaking at a graduation ceremony, I watched the university president hand diplomas to the seniors as they walked across the stage. What he said to each of them was simple but far more profound than he realized. He knew he had to keep the ceremony progressing, so he encouraged them to move quickly across the stage. As he gave them their degree, he said, "Congratulations. Keep moving." And so say I. Whatever you've done in your past—well done. Now keep moving.

Talk It Over

Fictional character Marleen Loesje said, "The longer you wait for the future, the shorter it will be."

1. In your opinion, what's the greatest reason students get stuck in their past?

2. Is there any memory or person that holds you back from embracing the future?

3. Talk about where your energy comes from—the past or the future. Why?

4. Can you name a time you saw a student break free from the rearview mirror and look ahead?

Assess Yourself

Assess yourself, using the criteria below, on a scale of 1–10 (1 being weak and 10 being strong).

a. I am keenly aware of where I get my energy
   1   2   3   4   5   6   7   8   9   10

b. I work through my struggle to overcome my fear of failure
   1   2   3   4   5   6   7   8   9   10

c. I maintain a healthy sense of adventure and anticipation
   1   2   3   4   5   6   7   8   9   10

d. I can celebrate the past, but I can let go of it to pursue the future
   1   2   3   4   5   6   7   8   9   10

Try It Out

Get in a quiet place with a pad of paper or a computer, and make a list of some of your favorite memories—experiences, achievements, friendships, etc. Make this a column on the left side of your document. Then take a moment to celebrate those memories. Seriously—relish the good times you've experienced in your past. Now make another list, on the right. This one should contain all the potential memories and accomplishments that could lie in front of you if you really put your mind to it. Let your imagination expand a bit. Consider the new environment you are now in, and dream of what could happen if you applied your time, your mind and your energy. Once you finish, compare the two lists. Both are something to enjoy—but ask yourself: Would you want to trade the right column for the left one? Consider what would happen if you did. What would your life look like if you only grasped what was behind you?

[A Compass or a GPS]

A Compass or a GPS

A GPS OR GOOGLE MAPS WILL BE HELPFUL ONLY IF YOU ARE ON PAVED ROADS. IF YOU ARE ENTERING NEW AREAS, YOU NEED A COMPASS THAT SHOWS YOU TRUE NORTH. SIMILARLY, WE NEED VALUES THAT PROVIDE DIRECTION WHEN WE ENTER NEW TERRITORY.

I bet you've used a Global Positioning System (a GPS) many times. If you travel to new places, you don't want to be without one. I travel all over the world—and I can tell you, my GPS has saved me on dozens of trips. Having this technology, we should never be lost again, at least in theory.

Years ago, when I first started using my GPS, I learned some good news and bad news about it. The good news is, no matter how much I deviate from the planned route, the GPS voice remains calm and poised. "She" never gets mad at me, calls me a jerk or gives up on me. She just says softly, "Rerouting." And then she somehow gets me to my destination.

The bad news about a GPS is—once in a while, when I'm in a completely foreign area with new roads or no roads, my system isn't very helpful. In other words, the GPS is great when there are commonly known streets and highways. A few years ago, however, I found myself in a remote part of Canada, where there were no signs, signals or paved roads. No maps were available for this territory, and my GPS was stumped. No landmarks or directions existed. I was, quite literally, in deep weeds. Modern tools could not help me navigate this new place—in fact, the only tool to guide me was a compass.

Have you ever used a compass before?

The compass is centuries old—as early as the Chinese Han Dynasty, two thousand years ago, the magnetic compass was invented. Chinese military used it for navigation around the year 1040. Western Europe began using compasses between 1187 and 1202. The compass is a device that needs no roads to provide direction, because it works by the earth's gravitational pull. When you look at a compass you can always see where "true north" is and follow its needle.

In the last century, we stopped using compasses because we got more sophisticated. We have freeways and signs; civilization and cell phones are everywhere; and now we have a GPS in our car. I'm convinced, however, that a compass is actually helpful as we progress into the future.

This is a picture of our life in periods of transition. Most of the time, our days are full of routines. We are creatures of habit. We develop ways of behaving, and we don't even have to think about it. Why? Because it's familiar territory. We know all the roads. When we find ourselves in new places, however, our routines evaporate. The GPS of our daily habits gets upset, and we need some kind of a "compass" to help us find our way in this new place.

This compass I am talking about is a set of personal values.

Personal values are like guidelines to live by. They are key words that contain ideals we want to live by, such as integrity, empathy, discipline, family and purpose. It was my sophomore year of college when I actually sat down for half a day and wrote down a list of six words that have since been my personal "core" values. They're words that define the most important priorities and principles I value in my life. This list remains on a wall next to my desk at home. Whenever I have a big decision to make—one that involves moving into new territory I've never been to before—I look at that list like it is a compass. It helps me remain the person I intend to be. Those values enable me to become the man I want to be when I'm old. They are not a "god," but a guide to help me make wise decisions when I'm tempted to react. Those values help me say yes and no to opportunities without guessing. Roy Disney once said, "It's not hard to make decisions when you know what your values are."[2]

Why are values relevant today? Our world keeps changing. We are mobile people. We love speed and convenience. Technology makes it easier to go new places and achieve new goals. The problem is—we're not always ethically or emotionally ready for these places. Innovation can take us to destinations that our character is not ready to experience. We are like Lewis and Clark drifting down the river…yet often without a compass. Years ago, Harold Lamb authored a book saying that Alexander the Great frustrated his men most often by leading them into uncharted territory. They continued moving into new lands where there were no maps—they literally had to draw the maps as they moved forward. Like those men, we are "marching off the map" today, going to places we've never been—technologically, morally and ethically; in business, and in government policy. Similarly, you are moving into new spaces where you've not been before. It would be easy to assume your days ahead will look just like the days before. But that's often not true. Yesterday's map won't do. Growing up, you likely had all kinds of people to tell you what to do or where to go next—a little like the voice on a GPS. The rules you were given were like roads you're instructed to drive on. At this point, there may be no paved roads. Now…you'll need a compass.

In February 2010, news came out that shocked sports fans everywhere. Golf legend Tiger Woods wasn't so squeaky clean after all. The reputation of this athlete, husband and father went south.

He had a car accident backing out of his driveway in the middle of the night. Later he was forced to confess to having multiple affairs with several women. Turns out this role model for kids was a playboy. I was disappointed as I watched the report on TV. Then I saw Tiger hold a press conference, where he explained everything. He acknowledged that what he had done was wrong. Next he shared how he'd left the values he'd been taught; he had felt he was above them. He then admitted he was wrong. His fame and talent had taken him to places he'd never been before—and he had no GPS for his lifestyle. And the compass his father had given him…well, he lost it. This left him to do whatever felt right, not what actually was right.

How Do We Find a Compass?

In order to be ready for new experiences, people and opportunities, I suggest you initiate the same exercise I did in college. Get some time alone and follow these steps:

1. Identify the Values in Your Life
Take a few hours and write out the words that describe your most important ideals and principles—the values that define the person you want to become. They can be nouns or adjectives. Then, add a statement that defines exactly what you mean by each word. Limit your list to six values.

2. Include Those Values in Your Decisions
Next, post those values where you can see them every day. Memorize them. Whenever you have a significant decision to make—one that's not black and white but perhaps a bit gray—consult those values. Do they guide you? Can you let them act as a consultant in the choices you make?

3. Implement Your Values in Your Routines
Finally, come up with actions that enable you to actually embody the values in your daily habits. This will help you immensely when you get outside of your daily habits. Your subconscious will take over and steer you in the best direction. You will naturally choose wisely.

In 2011, a statewide Iowa high school wrestling tournament made news when two girls qualified. But when Joel Northrup, the fifth-ranked wrestler in the state, was matched up to fight one of the girls, Cassy Herkelman, he refused. Northrup said he wouldn't wrestle because of his personal values. "Wrestling is a combat sport and it can get violent at times," he explained. "As a matter of conscience and my faith I do not believe that it is appropriate [for me to do it]…" His decision caused an uproar among teens and parents; everyone had an opinion on what was right. But it was Joel's decision to make, and he didn't want to treat females that way.[3]

What I love about Joel's statement is that he didn't say it was wrong for girls to wrestle. He simply said his values were guiding him away from wrestling a female. When he was in new territory, Joel's decision was clear, because he had a compass inside.

Do you?

Talk It Over

1. Why do you think it's difficult for most people to take a stand on controversial issues?

2. What are a few new areas you are facing now that will require tough decisions?

3. Talk about how you make hard choices when the issues are not black and white.

4. What are a handful of the personal core values you try to live by?

Assess Yourself

Assess yourself on each continuum below. Be honest as you place an X in the appropriate spot:

a. When faced with a new situation, I tend to:

|--|
Do what is easy and familiar to me   Do what seems to be wise even if it's hard

b. When I need to make a tough call, I tend to:

|--|
Look outside to others for an example   Look inside myself for what seems right

c. When I am in a group of people, I find I am most often:

|--|
A gps person   A compass person
I am prone to be a people pleaser   I am prone to find my own way

Try It Out

As soon as you can, find a quiet place and a pad of paper or a computer, and think about your own personal set of values. Companies have core values—why not people? As I suggested above, take a few hours and reflect on the principles you value most, the ones you want to guide the big decisions of your life—and write them down, along with a definition of what they mean to you. Then, find a community of close friends and talk the list over. Do you live by these principles?

A Bridge Not a Wall

EACH OF US ENCOUNTERS NEW AND DIFFERENT PEOPLE THROUGH LIFE. OUR NATURAL INCLINATION IS TO SEE DIFFERENCES AND PUT UP A WALL. WE'RE PRONE TO DISTRUST. WE MUST CONSCIOUSLY BUILD BRIDGES THAT CAN BEAR THE WEIGHT OF HONEST DISCLOSURE.

Did you ever watch the movie *Crash?* I saw it three times, and each time I was moved by this story of very different people's lives being woven together to benefit each other. What makes it even more powerful is that it's based on a real incident that took place in Los Angeles. The movie won Best Picture, Best Original Screenplay and Best Editing Awards at the 2005 Oscars.

In the film, the stories of several people from LA interplay: an African American LAPD detective estranged from his mother; his criminal younger brother, a gang associate; a District Attorney and his pampered and racist wife; a Persian-immigrant man who is wary of others; a police officer whose racism disgusts his young partner; an African-American Hollywood director and his wife, who encounter the racist officer; and a Hispanic named Daniel Ruiz. The film differs from other films about prejudice in its rather impartial approach to the issue. Rather than separating the characters into offenders and offended, victims of racism are often shown to be racist themselves in other situations. What struck me most in the film was seeing that people's perspectives often stemmed from ignorance and misconception rather than from malice.

The message of the story is simple but profound: We tend to push away people who are different, yet those people may be the very ones we most need in a critical moment of our lives. The fact is, this has probably happened to all of us. We are prejudiced. Do you remember what that word means? It's taken from two root words, meaning to *pre-judge*—to judge before fully experiencing the person. Believe it or not, we do this naturally. And it's not just about race.

Dr. Rebecca Bigler of the University of Texas created an experiment that demonstrates how quickly children develop "in-group" preferences and biases. Bigler gave T-shirts to three classes of preschool kids. Half of them wore blue shirts and half wore red ones, and they continued wearing them for three weeks.

According to authors Po Bronson and Ashley Merryman, "the teachers never mentioned their colors and never again grouped the kids by shirt color....Bigler wanted to see what would happen to the children naturally, once color groupings had been established." So, what was the result? "The kids didn't segregate in their behavior. They played with each other freely at recess. But when asked which color team was better to belong to, or which team might win a race, they chose their own color." They never showed hatred for the other team, says Bigler, but they did say things like "'Blues are fine, but not as good as us.' When Reds were asked how many Reds were nice, they'd answer 'All of us.' Asked how many Blues were nice, they'd answer 'Some.'"

Bigler's research shows that kids are "*developmentally* prone to in-group favoritism"; they're actually forming these preferences on their own, categorizing people, food, toys and more at a young age. Further, Bigler contends that once children identify someone as most closely resembling themselves, they like that person the most.[4] Bottom line?

- We naturally tend to hang around people who are similar .
- We are prone to like those who are like us.
- We tend to pre-judge those who are not like us.
- We tend to shy away from those who are different.

And even as we mature, we continue to lean toward what is familiar and what is comfortable. It takes less work to relate to someone who is just like me.

To put it another way, we tend to build bridges to reach those who are familiar, and walls to protect ourselves from those who are not. Consider this fact: In general, it is easier to build a fence than it is to build a bridge. In fact, most bridges require an engineer to get involved. They can be very complex—all the weight they have to hold, and the support they need to survive the traffic and the storms. Conversely, walls are relatively simple to construct. It's easy to build a lot of them.

The same is true with relationships. This is why we must be intentional about building bridges to those outside our "circle" of friends, those whose lifestyle, or personality, or background is...well, different. If we don't pursue them, it is possible we'll build a wall around ourselves and prevent them from getting too close. Especially when we find ourselves in new environments, we almost automatically find it easy to look for differences in others and put up a wall. Interaction on a deep level would be expensive. Plus—building a bridge is risky.

Daniel fell into this very trap his freshmen year in college. Feeling a little insecure, he deliberately found other guys in his residence hall who shared the same major, who all loved intramural sports, and who even liked the same food. He played it safe at first and only hung out with them. Then, a class project threw him into a group of students who were radically different. They came from different states and ethnic backgrounds, shared widely different political views, and had different gifts and interests. Daniel felt like a fish out of water.

Over time, however, he grew to appreciate these people. His predictable routines disappeared; he got exposed to all kinds of new interests, cool food and intriguing conversations. In the end, these students became best friends. They not only expanded him, but they influenced his major and shaped his career choice. In the end, Daniel told me this group saved his college career. You might say—he was forced to become a relationship engineer. He learned to build bridges.

A news report aired years ago about two men, Michael Weisser and Larry Trapp, who had an unlikely meeting that changed them both. Michael noticed families from a variety of ethnic backgrounds moving into his suburb of Lincoln, Nebraska, and decided to create welcome baskets to make them feel at home. Michael knew what it felt like to be an outsider and wanted to connect with them. Simultaneously, Larry Trapp, the Grand Dragon of the Ku Klux Klan, was breathing threats to every one of these minority families, telling them if they didn't move away within a month, he'd destroy their property. Larry was a bitter, violent man who, due to his diabetes, was confined to a wheelchair. Can you imagine the paradox of emotions these new people felt?

When Larry heard what Michael was doing, he called him and left a voicemail. He threatened his life if he didn't stop welcoming these "aliens" into town. Instead of withdrawing behind a wall, Michael decided to build a bridge. He called Larry up and told him, "I thought you should know I did some homework on you and discovered that you're confined to a wheelchair. I wondered if I could help you in some way. I'd be happy to swing over to pick you up and run errands with you if that could help—you know—groceries, dry cleaning, post office, whatever. Let me know." Larry Trapp didn't know what to say. How could a stranger offer this to a guy who just threatened him?

Eventually, the two connected, as Michael hoisted the paraplegic into his van and ran errands once a week for a month, until finally these two men…became friends. It ultimately transformed Larry Trapp's bitter view of both people and God. He denounced his involvement with the Ku Klux Klan and made amends to every family he'd threatened. The entire community was changed.[5]

You might say Michael was a relationship engineer, specializing in building bridges. And an entire community was better for it, including both Larry Trapp and Michael Weisser himself.

The fact is, we need to widen our circles and include others we are not yet comfortable with:

- We need others who are not like us to stretch us and force us to grow.

- We need them to be close enough to provide accountability and balance.

- We must build bridges of relationship with others that can bear the weight of truth.

Talk It Over

1. Why do you think most people build fences rather than bridges?

2. What makes building a relationship with a very different person challenging for you?

3. When it comes to relationships, technology is both a blessing and a curse. Talk about ways students must both overcome and capitalize on technology when bridge-building with new people.

4. Name the coolest relationship you've built with a very different person. What did you learn?

Assess Yourself

Assess yourself on the descriptions below. Be honest as you circle the most accurate word:

a. When I am faced with a crowd of new people, getting to know others is:

very easy   somewhat easy   depends on the person   somewhat hard   hard

b. When I need to get acquainted with a very different person, I tend to:

shy away   let them talk first   look for a natural connection   take initiative

c. When I am in a group of people, most of the time I tend to:

see the value of networking   follow the mood I am in   do what's most comfortable

Try It Out

This week, identify an event or an environment where there will be people who have different lifestyles or backgrounds than you. In other words, find a group of people unlike you. Come up with an appropriate way to participate, and purposefully meet three new people. Instead of focusing on being *interesting* to them, focus on becoming *interested* in them. Ask them questions about their family, their interests and their goals for the future. Make it natural, but get to know them. Then, reflect on paper what you learned about these new people and how you benefited from learning about them. Discuss it with your group.

IMAGE FOUR

[Baggage Fees]

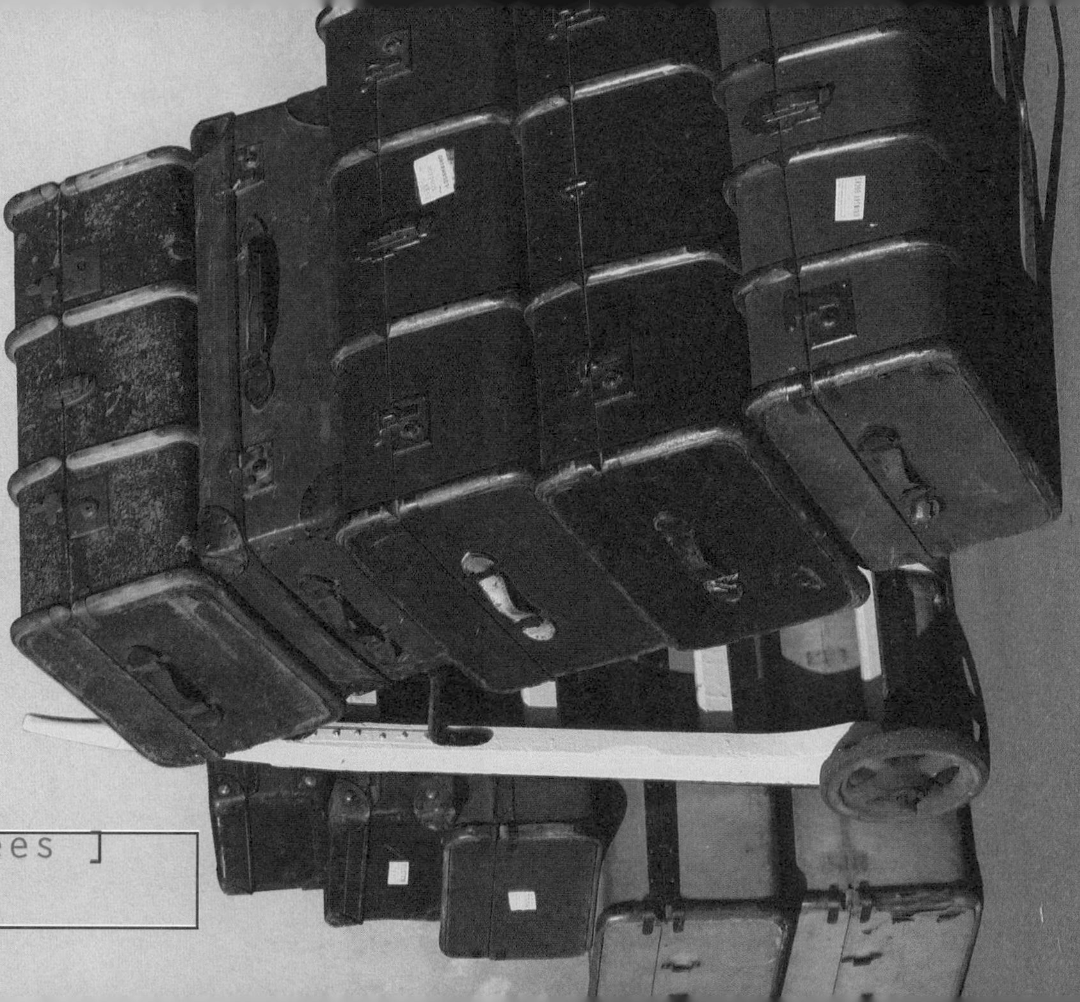

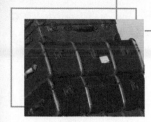

Baggage Fees

MOST CARS HAVE TRUNKS WHERE WE STORE LUGGAGE, BUT YOU CAN ONLY FIT SO MUCH. SOME OF US HAVE FAR TOO MUCH BAGGAGE. BAGS IN THE TRUNK CAN WEIGH US DOWN AND GET TOO BIG TO CARRY. ON FLIGHTS, BAGS CAN COST US. WE MUST DISCARD THEM SO THEY DON'T PREVENT US FROM MOVING FORWARD.

Last year, our family drove to Florida for our vacation. While it was a relaxing holiday, it was also a time for me to relearn a life lesson. As you can imagine, our automobile trunk was packed. Suitcases, cosmetic bags, video games and equipment, books and magazines to read, beach gear—you name it. We crammed it all in the trunk and backseat of our car. While it all fit—we faced two measurable consequences while traveling with all that luggage. First, it wasn't too comfortable being squeezed in the same place; we felt like sardines in a can. Second, our gas mileage was horrible. With all that weight in the back, we got far fewer miles per gallon than with no luggage.

In short, the volume of luggage we had:

- Made our drive crowded and chaotic.
- Made our travels slower and more difficult.
- Made our trip more expensive.

My guess is—you've noticed this same reality. The more baggage you have, the more bogged down you become. I've actually been on trips overseas when we had too much baggage. It was too heavy, and we had to determine what to leave behind. Actually, that's a great place to be. Choosing to leave some "stuff" behind makes the trip a little easier and swifter.

If you've flown anywhere, you know that airlines now charge you for checking luggage. Yep, they do everything they can to make a buck. The more bags you have, the more money you pay. It's something we now expect. This is why I try to follow a little rule when I fly anywhere, even overseas: I don't check any bags. I know if I've got baggage, it's gonna cost me.

This is not only a reality when traveling, it's a fact of life.

You are in a season of transition. Change is in the wind. You will find (if you haven't already) that if you carry emotional baggage with you—you are inviting problems. Unresolved conflicts, anger, relationship struggles at home, addictions, former partners where your status is still fuzzy, lack of forgiveness between you and a friend, insecurities, jealousy…you get the idea. These all count as excess baggage, and you can be sure they will weigh you down. In fact, they're going to cost you. Like our vacation, or like almost any flight you take, the baggage makes your trip cluttered and costly.

Psychiatrists Thomas Holmes and Richard Rahe once scoured the medical history of thousands of people. Their goal? They hoped to answer the question of whether stress might be linked to illness. In 1967, these two doctors published their results as the "Social Readjustment Rating Scale." Their findings include links between life changes, stress levels, and sickness. They look at shifts in our lives such as:

- Family separation/Leaving home
- Change in financial state
- Beginning or ending school
- Adjustment in personal routines
- Transition in schools or new friends
- Shift in sleeping habits

Holmes and Rahe report that all adjustments in our lives cause stress.[6] The level of stress parallels both the significance of each event and each person's adaptability. The two men also agree that the kinds of changes you've experienced as a student in transition can lead to baggage, if you don't handle them well.

Jeremy scored poorly on his first two science tests during his freshman year in high school. Mr. Steele, his teacher, noticed that Jeremy began to withdraw from him, refusing to accept any help to raise his scores. In November, Mr. Steele moved to a different school district. At this point, Jeremy spiraled into depression. He slept all the time, overate, and grew angry when people spoke to him. He told his mom he wanted to drop out of school. When he saw a counselor, Jeremy began to put his finger on why he was reacting so severely to his science class. His therapist discovered Jeremy had been abused by his father years earlier. When Jeremy was twelve, his dad had then left the family. Jeremy blamed himself. His poor performance in class, and his teacher vanishing, hit too close to home. The baggage from his past cost him dearly.

What's the Price of Our Baggage?

Tim O'Brien authored a famous book about the Vietnam War, called *The Things They Carried*. In it he describes the post-war realities veterans face. Most of the physical items soldiers carry are owned by the government, such as canteens, weapons and helmets. Troops return these to Uncle Sam when they return home. Unfortunately, the emotional bags they carry stay with them for years.

Today, it's not uncommon for former soldiers to confess they still feel unsafe without a weapon, even years after returning home. They'd conditioned themselves to be ready for the Taliban to storm through their doorway at any moment. They're constantly on edge. Some feel physical pain, which they can't explain since they were not physically wounded.

Explanations are now clear. In a recent study done with functional MRI (magnetic resonance imaging), researchers found that the same brain networks light up when you're burned with hot coffee and when someone you love leaves you. That is to say—there is no categorical difference between physical and emotional pain in the brain. The University of Michigan's Ethan Kross, PhD, says, "Heartache and painful breakups are 'more than just metaphors.'"[7] If we don't address the pain of our past, we may not have peace in the present.

Breaking Free from Emotional Bonds

This is why one important step of progress is to identify and free yourself from "excess baggage." Whatever your "life change units" are right now, one important action step is to handle them in a healthy manner. No distractions, no denial, but face reality and move on. Below is a table outlining four basic needs we all have. If these needs are unmet, we tend to do strange things to fill them:

Inward need:	If missing, we feel:	Common symptoms:
Belonging	Insecure	Overcompensation; emotional highs and lows
Worth	Inferior	Competition; self-doubt; need for recognition
Competence	Inadequate	Comparison with specific people; defensive attitude
Purpose	Insignificant	Compulsive, driven spirit; defeat; depression

So let me ask you some questions. Is there anything weighing you down? Are you distracted from your current goals by a past issue that lingers in your mind? Do you feel stuck? If so, below are some key questions to answer, and some assessments and action steps you can take.

Talk It Over

1. Do you think most students deal with their past "baggage" well? Why or why not?

2. Sometimes our culture distracts us from handling our baggage in a healthy way. What is it about our world today that makes it difficult to really be emotionally healthy?

3. True or False: Most of our "baggage fees" have to do with relationships. Why or why not?

4. Can you name a time when you identified an emotional need in your life and handled it well?

Assess Yourself

We commonly fall into "performance traps" when we have emotional baggage. We cope with our pain by reacting in the ways below. Circle the two most common ways you react to insecurities you face, then talk about them with your fellow students.

Coping Mechanisms:

Comparison – You compare yourself to others, keeping score in key areas of importance.

Condemnation – You judge others or yourself constantly, resulting in conceit or self-pity.

Control – To validate your worth, you feel you must take charge and protect your interests.

Compulsion – You're a people pleaser, driven to perform compulsively to gain others' approval.

Compensation – You feel like a victim and must now compensate for your losses or inferiority.

Competition – You become self-centered, determined to outdo others for attention or rewards.

Try It Out

If emotional baggage is causing you to feel "stuck," preventing you from facing a significant issue in your past, I suggest you see a counselor and talk it over. Also, the following steps are ones I have found helpful as I deal with the baggage of my day-to-day life:

1. **Review** – Take time to reflect on past issues and why you may feel "stuck" or discouraged.

2. **Recall** – Once an issue arises, think about how it made you feel and what you did.

3. **Release** – Surrender control of that issue or that person; let go of the past hurt.

4. **Reconcile** – If you need to return and talk to someone to make the issue right, do so.

5. **Request** – If you need direction or support, ask for help from a friend, a counselor or God.

6. **Refuse** – Choose to not allow wrong motives or past anger to rule you.

7. **Respond** – Return to a life of service and social connections. Serve from gratitude, not guilt.

IMAGE FIVE

Sturdy Guardrails

WE OFTEN DON'T NOTICE GUARDRAILS UNTIL WE NEED THEM. THEY KEEP US ON THE ROAD DURING A CURVE OR DANGEROUS SPOT. SIMILARLY, WE MUST PLACE GUARDRAILS IN OUR LIVES—BOUNDARIES OR PEOPLE WHO KEEP US FROM DAMAGING OURSELVES WITH POOR DECISIONS.

I will never, ever forget a trip to Sri Lanka years ago. I was with a team of leaders late one night, as we rode in a van up a steep mountain pass. The path was winding around the side of the mountain, and it was dark. All six of us on board grew scared because our driver was speeding along the road—at 60 miles an hour—and there were no guardrails. It was surreal.

As we raced around a bend, I peered over the cliff to see what was down below. I saw the lights of buildings hundreds of feet down. It was at this point I developed a great appreciation for those little things we call guardrails. I had never prayed so hard in my life. Fortunately, we made it.

If you think about it, guardrails are something no one really notices…until we need them. That night in Sri Lanka, I would have paid dearly for some fence or barrier to protect our van from tumbling over the edge.

My friend Andy once spoke on this subject and shared the official definition of guardrails:

> Guardrail: a system designed to prevent travelers from straying into dangerous or off-limit territory.

He used this as a metaphor just as I will in this chapter. In our lives, we need guardrails. We need something or someone to keep us from drifting or speeding over an edge that's dangerous. They can be *people,* or they can be *standards* we set for ourselves, but at some point, every person in this world will need them to stay on track. In fact, as I look back on my life, every bad decision I now regret was the result of my failure to put guardrails in place to protect me.

Let's explore this image a bit further. Guardrails are positioned in four places:

1. Where the road curves. (They ensure we don't veer off as our path changes.)

2. Where there is a bridge. (They keep us from driving off the road into water.)

3. Where there are medians. (They keep us from drifting into oncoming traffic.)

4. Where there are cliffs. (They keep us from falling and crashing down below.)

When we invite people in our life to be "guardrails," they're most important when we face the same junctions: when our path changes, when we may fall and crash, and when we encounter treacherous people moving in the opposite direction. The value of a guardrail is simple: It is better to bump up against a guardrail and cause a little damage, than to drive off the road and cause huge damage—and maybe even kill ourselves. It makes sense. In my life, I meet with two fellow leaders who are like guardrails to me. I have given them permission to ask me questions about my personal habits and lifestyle, my goals, my financial decisions, my friends and family, and so on. I realize this may sound strange, but I actually invite them to hold me accountable—to doing what I mean to do. To keeping my commitments. Why? Because I have had a tendency to drift. I may have the best of intentions, but I can still get distracted or lazy, or just make stupid decisions.

You've likely heard of Victor Hugo. He wrote some of the most famous stories in history, like *Les Miserables* and *The Hunchback of Notre Dame*. He was brilliant. But he was also very distracted. It took him seventeen years to finish the story of *Les Miserables*. Instead of writing, he'd wander through the streets, talk to people, mess around in his garden—you name it. Anything but finish the story. His friends kept insisting that he complete it, but he just couldn't discipline himself to do it. Until he put a guardrail in place: One day, he asked his servant to do something strange. He told him that once he'd fallen asleep, he wanted the servant to come into his room and take his clothes. That would force him to stay in his room…and write. Only after a full day of writing could his servant return his clothes so that he could go outside and talk to his friends. It was this guardrail that enabled him to finish *Les Miserables*—and the world has benefited greatly.

I recognize the idea of inviting people to remind you of what you should do sounds strange. Our culture certainly does not appreciate this. We want our freedom. Accountability almost feels like having another parent around. But that's not it at all. It's about being convinced of a standard of behavior you want to embrace—then putting people around you to protect you from drifting from it. These relationships are close and transparent. Vulnerable. They can be like roadside assistance on your journey, offering words of support when you need them. Years ago, an experiment was conducted to measure people's capacity to endure pain. The goal was to see how long a barefooted person could stand in a bucket of ice water. It was discovered that when there was someone else present offering encouragement and support, the person standing in the ice water could tolerate pain twice as long as when no one was present. Guardrails help you live the life you've always wanted, because someone else is there to provide rest stops along the way.

It might not surprise you, but when people fail to place guardrails in their lives, they can be carried along by their self-absorbed ambitions, jealousy, lust, greed and egos. When we're in this emotional state—we can't even see our vulnerability. We're blinded by our desires. In the northern parts of Canada and Alaska, the Eskimos have graphic methods for capturing wolves. They coat a knife with blood and freeze it. Once the first coat of blood is frozen, they add a second and third coat in the same way. Then they place the knife in the icy ground, blade up. In the middle of the night, when the wolves smell the blood, they approach it and begin licking it off the blade. By the time they get past the first layer, they are consumed with the taste. Eventually, in their attempt to get every drop, they begin cutting their own tongues and licking their own blood. By morning, the wolves are found lying dead on the ice.[8] They did it to themselves. At the risk of sounding gross—sometimes we're like the wolves. We're our own worst enemies.

Sometimes we need someone to be a guardrail. A person to help us develop healthy habits, attitudes and routines. Self-control. Balance. Clear direction. These guardrail people provide:

1. Support

2. Guidance

3. Accountability

Businesses understand the need for this, so they create a board of directors. So do churches and non-profit organizations. So let me ask you a question: Why not you and me? Why not establish a personal board of directors—a group of people, or even one person—that you invite to ask tough questions of you and keep you aligned with your purpose? What if you invited these people to get coffee and asked them to meet with you regularly? In these meetings, give them a list of questions you want them to ask you each time you meet. Then, commit to yourself to be totally honest in your answers. Invite them to watch your progress.

When I was a freshman in high school, I ran on our track team. A few of us would run together at practice every afternoon, while the cheerleaders were also practicing near the track. I noticed that when we ran by the cheerleaders, every one of us guys looked better. We took on great form, we threw our chests out, sucked our stomachs in and looked like Olympians. Why? We knew we were in front of these girls… who just might be watching. It was hilarious.

The truth is—we all do better when we are watched. If we know someone is observing us, checking on us and noting our progress, we tend to perform better. It's been said, "The doctor who has himself as his doctor…has a lousy doctor." We need other people who serve us as guardrails.

Talk It Over

1. Why do you think most relationships remain superficial and never reach the depths of this kind of accountability? Why do people tend to "stick to the surface"?

2. Think about our society today. What are some obvious consequences of people failing to put guardrails in their lives?

3. If you had a guardrail person in your life (maybe you already do), what questions would you need them to ask you? In what areas do you most need accountability and support?

4. Who is someone you could invite to be a guardrail person in your life?

Assess Yourself

Below is a list of "gifts" that an accountability partner (guardrail person) provides. Which ones do you need most in your life right now? Circle the three most tangible needs you have:

1. Affirmation – Words of encouragement

4. Accountability – Words of prompting

2. Assessment – Words of evaluation

5. Acceptance – Words of belief

3. Advice – Words of direction

6. Admonishment – Words of correction

Now talk about your responses. Why did you circle those needs?

Try It Out

This action step is obvious. If you don't already have a personal "board of directors" who act as guardrails in your life, identify a person or community of people who could play this role. They should be people who:

1. You have a safe and close relationship with.
2. You believe will be objective and forthright with you.
3. You know support you and believe in your potential.
4. You are willing to be transparent and completely honest with.
5. You can access quickly because they are geographically close.

Next, meet with them and invite them to perform the role of a guardrail person. (You may decide to both play this role for each other.) Then, create a list of personal questions you need them to ask you on a regular basis. These questions are generally ones you would not invite just anyone to talk to you about. Some will be very personal—but they are about issues that matter to you. Finally, set up your first meeting in a safe place where you feel comfortable to have this conversation.

IMAGE SIX

[Tollbooths
or Roadblocks]

Tollbooths or Roadblocks

IN LIFE, SOME CHALLENGES REQUIRE US TO RISE TO THE OCCASION. MANY ARE UNAVOIDABLE. THEY WILL EITHER BECOME TOLLBOOTHS WE PROGRESS THROUGH, OR ROADBLOCKS. SOMETIMES IT'S LIKE A ONE-WAY ROAD—YOU CAN ONLY GO ONE DIRECTION. WE MUST PAY THE TOLL.

No one likes embarrassing moments…but every one of us has them. I've had my share of embarrassing moments. One of them took place a few years back when I drove up to a tollbooth on a freeway without any money. Ugh. The toll was just fifty cents, but I had nothing in my wallet except credit cards. I was stuck. I was running late for a meeting; I needed to make progress, and that silly gate stopped me. I'm sure you would have been entertained that day by watching me try to negotiate my way past the tollbooth with the lady who was taking the cash. I tried everything, from writing a check to promising I'd come back and pay her later. But alas, the tollbooth had became a roadblock. I didn't have what it took, and she would not let me pass through. I had to borrow the money from the guy behind me. What a humiliating moment for me.

For many of us, this is a picture of life. As we move through various stages of our lives, we reach junctions—points of transition—where we must shift gears and slow down. Suddenly, we realize we have to pay a price to proceed. It's like a tollbooth. The price might be a tough decision we must make or a situation we must leave behind; it may mean a class we must take or a job we must quit. It could be anything that is costly to us. It's at these moments that we discover that the junction will either become a tollbooth or a roadblock. We either choose to pay the price…or we can't find it in ourselves to do what is hard. And we get stuck, just like me on that freeway.

Let me illustrate with one important example. Over the last several years, many teens and twenty-somethings have gotten stuck. They can't seem to progress through adolescence. Several college deans have said to me, "26 is the new 18." Kids are often unprepared for adulthood. It's like many don't want to leave their childhood. The tollbooth has become a roadblock. I am picking up evidence that this is a worldwide phenomenon. Listen to the proof:

page 37

- In one survey, students indicated that the event that marks the beginning of adult responsibility is…"having my first child."[9] Hmmm. Americans aren't doing this until age 27.

- In 2006, 60% of students moved back home after finishing college. In 2009, that number had risen to 80%.[10] It's more than a bad economy. They're not career-ready.

- Condoleezza Rice and Joel Klein report that three out of four teens are not even fit to serve in the military because they are obese, didn't graduate high school or have criminal records.[11]

- The MacArthur Foundation funded a research project that said for many kids, the transition into adulthood doesn't occur until 34 years of age.[12]

By the way, I don't fault students for this. We adults have failed to get them ready for life after leaving home. We have done more protecting than preparing. In some ways, we have created a "postponed generation." The good news is—it doesn't have to be this way. I know many students who have shocked everyone by leaping forward, who exceeded everyone's expectations in school, at work, in their creativity, and most importantly, in their maturity.

Have you heard of Malala? She is a perfect example of a young leader who faced roadblocks on her way to her goal. Malala Yousafzai lives in Pakistan. As a teenager, she saw the need to help other kids get an education in a country where so many are denied—especially girls. So she took a stand, spoke out, wrote articles and raised money to help underprivileged kids get into school and graduate. Soon, she became known and acquired both fans and enemies. The Taliban is still alive and well in that part of the world. One day, a Taliban terrorist stopped a bus that Malala and other students were aboard, and demanded that she step off the bus. When she did—she was shot in the face. Three bullets flew and Malala was severely injured leaving her in critical condition. When word got out, many assumed Malala would not survive this attack—but she did. Afterward, many assumed that would go silent in her Taliban infested territory—but she came back stronger than ever. In fact she wrote: "The terrorists thought they would change my aims and stop my ambitions, but nothing changed in my life except this: weakness, fear and hopelessness died. Strength, power and courage was born … I am not against anyone, neither am I here to speak in terms of personal revenge against the Taliban or any other terrorist group. I'm here to speak up for the right of education for every child. I want education for the sons and daughters of the Taliban and all terrorists and extremists."

On Malala's 16th birthday, July 12, 2013, she spoke these words to the United Nations to call for worldwide access to education. At age 17 she become the youngest winner of the Nobel Peace Prize in history. Her story is amazing. It never would have happened, however, if this teen never learned how to turn a roadblock into a tollbooth. She paid the price and is making progress better than ever.

In 1962, Victor & Mildred Goertzel published a book called *The Cradles of Eminence*, a study of 415 high-performing people. The authors spent years attempting to understand what led to their greatness, and they searched for similarities in the stories of these outstanding and famous people.

Can you guess what they found?

The most stunning fact was that 392 of the 415 people had endured great obstacles on the way to becoming who they were.[13] That's 95% of the incredible performers! They had paid the toll by perseverance, determination and overcoming obstacles—that is, by choosing to pay the price.

So, let me ask you a question: In what area are you stuck right now? Why have you stalled? I've found I often stop moving forward when I feel like a victim of my circumstances. In other words, when I feel I have no choice in a matter, that I'm forced to do what someone else wants me to do, I may unintentionally stop progressing. The fact is, it may be true that there's only one option ahead. Sometimes the tollbooths we face are on a "One Way" road. We have no choice but to pay the price. But that doesn't mean we have no choice in the matter. Never assume that. This is when we get to decide just *how* we will travel. In short, you may not get to choose *where you go*, but you always get to choose *how you'll travel*. We can decide to engage our challenges with passion, to fully commit to a goal, to compete with our past and improve, to overcome the setbacks we face, and to enjoy the journey along the way.

Do you remember the story about the old donkey that fell in a deep well? Its owner felt horrible but saw no solution. Rescue seemed impossible. Finally, the farmer concluded that, well, the animal was old, and the well did need to be filled in—so maybe he should just bury the donkey and be done with it. The farmer asked some neighbors to help, and before long they were all shoveling dirt into the well. When the donkey realized what was happening, it whimpered and struggled. Then suddenly, the noise stopped. The farmer peered into the well and discovered that the donkey was still alive, and rising toward him! It had discovered that if it simply shook the new dirt off, instead of becoming covered with earth, it could step on top of the dirt and eventually climb out of the well.

Just as we must not get too comfortable sitting at the tollbooth, we cannot get comfortable with dirt all over us. We must shake it off and pay the price of the challenge before us. In short, we must be willing to leave what is comfortable to pursue what is compelling. Are you willing?

Talk It Over

1. Why do students and other young adults get stuck, in your opinion?

2. Do you remember the story of Peter Pan? He was from Neverland, where no one grows up. What elements in our culture play into this "Neverland" syndrome?

3. What is the number one "roadblock" you face today?

4. What is the price you believe you'll need to pay?

Assess Yourself

Below, list two important challenges you face. Then, rate yourself on the scale under each one.

1. Challenge One: _____

I'm stalled **1   2   3   4   5   6   7   8   9   10** I'm progressing

2. Challenge Two: _____

I'm stalled **1   2   3   4   5   6   7   8   9   10** I'm progressing

Try It Out

Donald Miller blogs about this idea and explains that he sees challenges and conflict as brilliant helpers. He suggests they're great because almost "every good thing in life" comes to us when we're "not satisfied with something else. Dissatisfied with debt," he says, we create a budget. Discontent with loneliness, we join a community. Miller then furnishes some steps we can take to face challenges.[14] I've included some of his thoughts below, with my own added commentary:

1. Don't play a victim and act like problems aren't supposed to happen. Tough times are normal, and they happen to everyone. They are not going away, so get used to them.

2. Don't give in to wishful thinking. There is no use wishing a problem away. It's a waste of time. Denial never solved any problem, nor did wishing or pretending. Only action does.

3. Take action. Discover what you can do to face the challenge…even if it's just one step. Run to the roar. Don't wait for a warm feeling. As Nike says, "Just do it."

4. Don't be afraid to cause more conflict. Perhaps you need to make a tough decision that will affect others, but which you know is right. Pay the price. Say and do what you must to progress.

5. Make a list of how this challenge is making you better. Don't miss what you learn and how you grow from this problem.

international arrivals - terminal 1   16:44

flight	origin	time	status
SW 856	EROS	19:50	
SA1758	WINDHOEK	20:10	
SW 744	WINDHOEK	20:40	
BA 059	LONDON-HEATHROW	08:05+	
QR 580	DOHA	08:30+	
SA 221	LONDON-HEATHROW	09:30+	
SW 742	WINDHOEK	12:45+	
SA1722	WALVISBAAI	15:10+	
SA1754	WINDHOEK	15:10+	

IMAGE SEVEN
[Flight Delay]

international arrivals - terminal 1   16:44

flight	origin	time	status
SW 856	EROS	18:50	
SA1758	WINDHOEK	20:10	
SW 744	WINDHOEK	20:48	
BA 059	LONDON-HEATHROW	08:05+	
QR 580	DOHA	08:30+	
SQ 221	LONDON-HEATHROW	09:30+	
SW 742	WINDHOEK	12:45+	DELAY
SA1722	WALVISBAAI	15:10+	
SA1754	WINDHOEK	15:10+	

Flight Delay

EXPERIENCED TRAVELERS KNOW THEY'RE NOT IN COMPLETE CONTROL. DELAYS OCCUR, STORMS ERUPT AND INTERRUPTIONS HAPPEN. SIMILARLY, WE MUST CALIBRATE OUR EXPECTATIONS, MANAGE DISAPPOINTMENTS AND BE REALISTIC ABOUT THE SPEED AND EASE OF OUR LIVES.

Like many executives, I travel all over the world. This year, I will speak at 125 events somewhere on Planet Earth. I love it…except for one thing. Flight delays. Ugh. I hate them. I wish I could tell you I am a very patient person, but alas, I am not…yet.

These delays happen half the time I travel, so you'd think I'd be better at dealing with them. One might think I could even psych myself up to expect them or even prepare for them—but I don't. Recently, I showed up at my airport gate in Atlanta only to find the flight had been delayed for 30 minutes. I thought, *OK. I can handle that.* I would still make my connection and fulfill my responsibilities that night in Oklahoma. But after 35 minutes, we were still standing around the gate. No further word. Obviously, we were going to be there a bit longer. Finally, the gate agent told us that it would just be a few more minutes. Everyone remained hopeful. Soon, however, our hope vanished, as we stood around for another 45 minutes. Several people started making calls, hoping to catch other flights or cancel their plans. I had pulled out my phone to change my plans, when the agent said over the intercom, "The inbound plane has landed. We will be boarding soon." My hopes were fanned into flame. But then…we waited some more. No airplane. After 25 minutes passed, I asked the agent when she thought we'd take off. She replied:

"Just a few more minutes."

At this point, I didn't believe her. Unfortunately, however, the airline kept all of us hanging on to the expectation that we'd be leaving soon. It didn't happen. In fact, within an hour they finally told us, "The flight's been canceled."

I cannot tell you how frustrated I was that someone didn't just get honest with us and suggest we make other plans. By the time I tried to do so, there were no more options. I was stuck.

Does this little scenario sound familiar?

This scene is another picture of life, especially when we are living in seasons of transition. We begin with a certain expectation. Often, we're excited about the new chapter that will soon begin in our lives. We anticipate. Inevitably, though, something will happen that we didn't expect. Our journey is delayed. We have to wait. People are vague and can't tell us what's going on. We get stuck. Maybe it was a class we tried to register for that suddenly closed. Maybe it was the hope of making a team, or a sorority or a fraternity. Perhaps it was a teacher we'd hoped to get, but didn't. It might be an internship we applied for, or a job opening or promotion we felt we deserved. It could be a relationship that suddenly evaporated or an opportunity that fell through. Somehow, the best-laid plans can fail. Life shifts. We find that we're not in control.

It's been said a thousand times, and I believe it's true: Life is pretty much about managing expectations. The people who are well-adjusted and happiest are not without expectations, but they are people who are adaptable. Like a good sailor, they've learned to adjust the sails with the winds, so they can still get to the destination they've targeted.

Decades ago, two young men contracted a disease that was terrifying at the time: polio. Before the polio vaccine, it was one of the most deadly and disabling illnesses in America. These guys were friends…and now had something new in common. Once they got the disease, however, their lives took two different directions. The first man became very depressed by his diagnosis. It was understandable. He would have to spend his life in a wheelchair, unable to do the things most guys love to do—play sports, enjoy work, spend time with females and eventually have a normal family. Over time he grew bitter and slipped into a self-absorbed life. The second young man, however, decided not to grow resentful over his condition. He had chosen to go into public service and felt that maybe…just maybe…his painful condition could help him relate to those less fortunate than him. He remained involved in his community and later was elected to public office. You've likely never heard of the first man. You do know the second one: President Franklin D. Roosevelt.

From Illusion to Disillusion

Sadly, today, many of us become depressed so easily. We give up too quickly when things don't go as we had hoped. Our confident, idealistic childhoods full of trophies and ribbons give way to cynicism far too many times. Too many young people are experiencing deep disillusionment.

A long-time mentor shed some light on this for me recently. He reminded me that a person can't become disillusioned unless they're first "illusioned." By this he meant that when we have illusions about reality—that's when we are vulnerable to cynicism.

Whether it's an illusion about a perfect marriage, or about church people being nice, or about the job market always providing good income for college graduates, we need someone to help us manage our expectations.

Reality eventually raises its ugly head. If we've been conditioned to have some idealistic expectations, we'll acquire an illusion about happiness, convenience, speed or simplicity, and can then spiral downward. Far too frequently, parents, teachers, coaches and youth workers haven't prepared kids for a difficult future as adults; in fact, we've painted a far too idealistic picture of reality. The truth is... life is often hard. We're not in control. My question for adults is this: Are we setting kids up for disillusionment because of the illusions we feed them?

We must strike a balance. Tonya Hurley wrote, "If you expect nothing, you can never be disappointed. Apart from a few starry-eyed poets or monks living on a mountaintop somewhere, however, we all have expectations. We not only have them, we need them. They fuel our dreams, our hopes, and our lives like some super-caffeinated energy drink."[15] The best solution, then, is to learn adaptability—to be like a tree that can bend with the wind in a storm. We must balance how we possess expectations, but also realize that a wonderful gift may not be wrapped as we expect.

The truth is, expectations influence us constantly. Not only do our expectations play a huge role in our contentment and our performance, other's expectations of us play a gigantic role too.

Dr. Wayne Dyer tells of an "accidental" experiment that took place during the 1960s. In one class, the teacher's roster included the students' IQ test scores. In another class, the teacher got a similar roster, but the students' locker numbers were mistakenly included in place of their IQ scores. This teacher thought the locker numbers were her students' actual IQ scores.

A year later, some interesting facts turned up: In the class without the mixed-up roster, kids with higher IQs had done better than kids with lower IQs. That's predictable. But in the other class, "students with higher locker numbers scored significantly higher than those with lower locker numbers!"[16]

Is this a coincidence? I don't think so. We are tangibly impacted by the expectations of our leaders and teachers. Furthermore, we tend to relate to others based on how we expect them to perform or behave in return. What if we chose not to tie our expectations to fate, but to faith in others and in ourselves…and chose at the same time to remain flexible?

A friend told me recently that he met a former pole-vaulter from the Ukraine. The athlete had set a record in his time by vaulting 21 feet. Incredible. My friend asked him how he did it, when others had tried and failed many times. The man smiled and replied, "It's easy. My coach always told me I could vault 22 feet. So that's what I aimed for."

Talk It Over

1. Talk about your perspective on expectations. Do they play a huge role in your life?

2. Why do you think people "crash and burn" when they don't get something they want?

3. Discuss an expectation you had that didn't pan out. How do you handle unmet expectations?

Assess Yourself

Below, define the three areas where you struggle the most with unfulfilled expectations. Talk about why:

1. Expectation: _____

This a struggle because...

2. Expectation: _____

This a struggle because...

3. Expectation: _____

This is a struggle because...

Try It Out

Choose one disappointment in your past and type it or write it down. Perhaps it was an expectation you had hoped would play out. On the same page, write out what you had hoped for, why it was so important to you, and why you feel it didn't turn out that way. Then, address the most important part: Write down what you believe is the healthiest way for you to respond to the situation at this point. What adjustments must you make? Talk it over.

IMAGE EIGHT
[Pass on the Left]

IMAGE EIGHT
[Pass on the left]

Pass on the Left

IN LIFE, YOU WILL NOTICE THAT THE PEOPLE YOU ONCE HUNG AROUND MAY NOT CONTINUE WITH YOU ON YOUR JOURNEY. THAT'S OK. WHEN YOU GROW IN NEW DIRECTIONS, BE SURE TO PASS OTHERS APPROPRIATELY, MAKING SURE YOU BURN NO BRIDGES ALONG THE WAY.

I spoke with an old college roommate recently. He told me he felt guilty about not staying in touch with our old buddies from school. To be truthful, we both felt badly. Those were good times, and the guys were fun to hang around. There was one particular person who came up in our conversation. His name was Casey. My roommate hadn't talked to Casey in years, and now—he felt like a horrible friend. When I probed him with questions, however, I saw what had really happened. Casey was needy. There's nothing wrong with that, but Casey was always asking something of everyone: requesting loans he never repaid; needing attention; wanting to borrow clothes or cars; or wanting some referral or endorsement for a job. All the conversations and transactions were one-way: Casey was the receiver; everyone else, the giver. He only contacted you when he needed something. With all his own responsibilities at home and work, my roommate eventually wasn't able to give Casey any more time, money or attention. You might say my roommate "broke up" with his friend. They were simply in two different places.

This sparked an interesting concept I want to share in this chapter. In life, you will notice that the people you once hung around may not continue with you on your journey. That's OK. While it's important to cultivate friendships, it is impossible to stay "close" to everyone, and I believe you don't need to feel guilty about it. People will intersect our lives for a season and for a reason, and we should enjoy that intersection. At the same time, most of the people I hung around 20 years ago are not the ones I am with today. None of them are poor friends—our lives have just gone in different directions. Social media makes it easier to stay in touch, but evidence suggests that, still, the average person cannot maintain real relationships with more than 150 people.[17]

Thanks to Facebook, "de-friending" is easy. With one push of a button we can stop those unwanted people from showing us their vacation photos or life updates. (Bill Gates, CEO of Microsoft, flat out quit Facebook in 2009 because he had "too many friends."[18]) But this act was around long before Facebook. Psychologists consider the process of "de-friending" an "inevitable life stage, a point where people achieve enough maturity and self-awareness to know who they are and what they want out of their remaining years." They "have a degree of clarity about which friends deserve full attention and which are a drain."

Reporter Alex Williams of *The New York Times* explains: "The winnowing process even has a clinical name: socioemotional selectivity theory, a term coined by Laura L. Carstensen, a psychology professor who is the director of the Stanford Center on Longevity….Dr. Carstensen's data show that the number of interactions with acquaintances starts to decline after age 17…and then picks up again between 30 and 40 before starting to decline sharply from 40 to 50." In short, people move from being explorers and collectors of friends to being miners who dig for a few nuggets of gold.[19]

Survey Says…

Our problem is, we often don't know how to walk away from a relationship in a healthy way. A survey by *TODAY.com* discovered that of respondents, over three quarters "said they'd had a toxic friend at some point." For a third of them, it had actually been a best friend.[20] Somehow, we stay close to "frenemies" because it's just too tough to end the relationship.

Here's some good advice: When you recognize someone who won't finish the journey with you, or when you grow in new directions, be sure to "pass" others appropriately. Make sure you burn no bridges along the way. It's OK to not stay close to everyone. Friends come and go. While many people don't know how to cultivate a healthy friendship, even more don't know how to end one. There is a right way and a wrong way to end a relationship. Before we examine some steps for accomplishing this, let's review the toxic friendships we should consider cutting:

The False Victim: Eventually, these people will actually try to say you're hurting them. Victims always feel under attack by somebody; they want to be rescued. Some people want to be victims so they "don't have to take responsibility for their lives," explains Donald Miller.

The Narcissist: These people appear to be friends, but they're really in love with themselves. They're self-absorbed and are always talking about "me, myself and I." They often fail to see the needs and importance of anyone else. It's all about them.

The Chronic Downer: Like "Debbie Downer" from *Saturday Night Live,* these people always see the negative side of life; they are not happy, life is scarce, and things are sure to go wrong. They seem to sap the fun out of almost every situation, and they are critics of everything.

The Bully: Donald Miller says the quickest way to spot bullies is to see what they laugh at. You'll notice they laugh not at themselves, but at others; they make fun of others but are not self-deprecating. This isn't healthy. Bullies manipulate people so they can look good.

The Underminer: These people are hard to spot at first. They're nice to your face and seem to like you, but behind your back—they undermine your friendship. They gossip and backbite. In reality, they try to pit friends against friends to make themselves look good. They're two-faced.

The Flake: Sadly, these people may promise you everything, but they fail to come through on their promises. They flake out on commitments, appointments, pledges and dates. Eventually, they lose the trust of others. No one can depend on them.

The Overly Religious: These people are all about controlling others. They use Bible verses to prove they're right and others are wrong. They aren't healthy people who are devoted in their faith; they're trying to take advantage of their religion to give themselves authority. It's unhealthy.

"All of this may sound calloused, but as we get older, we realize there are people in the world who refuse to mature," says author Donald Miller, who inspired part of the list above. "Maturity means we are honest, safe and transparent. A mature person understands their faults and admits to them. An immature person is looking for power in some kind of game. If you want to be mature, surround yourself [with] mature people."[21]

So Who Do You Let Stay Close to You?

When you spend time with various people this year, ask yourself the following questions:

Do I feel better after spending time with them?

Do they bring out the best in me? Are they a positive influence?

When I haven't been in touch, how do I feel?

Do we both make an effort?

Do they celebrate my successes?

How Do You Break a Friendship in a Healthy Way?

For many relationships, it is simply OK to move forward in your life without declaring you are leaving them "behind." For others, however, you may have a close relationship that needs to be redefined. So, how does that conversation look? In Dr. Henry Cloud's book, *Necessary Endings*, he offers suggestions for how to end a relationship:

1. Begin with the end in mind. Know exactly the conclusion you must reach that's healthy for you.

2. Be caring but truthful. It's easy to fudge the truth when you don't want to hurt someone.

3. Practice and role-play if necessary. Rehearse what you'll say; write it out if you need to.

4. Get the tone right. Don't be harsh, angry or shaming—be caring and empathetic.

5. Validate the relationship and the person. Be clear about how you value them as a person.

6. Get agreement. When a topic is emotional, it's important to be clear about the needed change.

7. Deal with defensive reactions. Don't let their anger get you off track. Be decisive and controlled.

8. You may need others. If it's a difficult person, bring another friend along for support.[22]

Talk It Over

1. We live in a very "social" world. How is it that people often fail to be good at friendships?

2. Can you recall a time when you and a friend went separate ways? How did you handle it?

3. Why is it important to not burn bridges with others? Can you recall a time you didn't burn a bridge and later were glad you didn't?

Assess Yourself

Below, assess yourself on how you typically handle relationships in your life:

Characteristic:	Never									Always

1. I tend to try to hang on to every friendship forever:
   1 2 3 4 5 6 7 8 9 10

2. I have difficulty confronting unhealthy relationships.
   1 2 3 4 5 6 7 8 9 10

3. I enjoy friends but find it easy to exit friendships.
   1 2 3 4 5 6 7 8 9 10

4. I often mishandle broken relationships, making enemies.
   1 2 3 4 5 6 7 8 9 10

5. I'm able to allow people to come and go in my life.
   1 2 3 4 5 6 7 8 9 10

Try It Out

Choose three relationships in your life that represent one of these scenarios:

1. A relationship you let go of, but not well.

2. A relationship you have not let go of, but where you should now "pass on the left."

Now, write down how you will respond to each of these scenarios. For example, in the first scenario, perhaps you need to contact this person and apologize for the way you handled the relationship. See if you can mend any hurt from the past. In the second scenario, jot down how you will move forward but not burn any bridges in the relationship (unless it's toxic); determine to do it in a healthy way. Once you determine your game plan, talk it over with your community.

1/2

F

Tank Half-Full or Empty?

Tank Half Full or Empty?

IT'S AN AGE-OLD QUESTION: IS IT HALF-EMPTY OR HALF-FULL? THE ANSWER IS BOTH, DEPENDING ON WHETHER YOU'RE EMPTYING IT OR FILLING IT. IN LIFE, WE MUST REPLACE DISCONTENTMENT, WHERE WE SEE THINGS AS HALF-EMPTY, WITH DISSATISFACTION, WHERE WE STRIVE TO FILL THINGS MORE.

In the early days of the NFL, Joe Namath was "the man." He was the star quarterback for the New York Jets, and he predicted his team would upset the favored Baltimore Colts in 1969's Super Bowl III—and they did. Namath was the epitome of a superstar, but you probably know only part of his story. He played college football for the University of Alabama. He was drafted before he graduated and chose to do what many talented athletes do—forgo graduation and play professionally. Joe didn't disappoint anyone with his pro career. Years later, however, it bothered "Broadway Joe" that he had never finished his degree. He had attempted it over the years, but something had always gotten in the way. So he called the University of Alabama athletic department and asked my friend Kevin Almond what it would take for him to graduate. Kevin walked him through the process, and Namath became a college graduate. He did it. He completed his degree at 64 years old.

What I love about this story is—Joe didn't need a bachelor's degree to move forward in his career at that point. He was a star. He had money. He's in the Hall of Fame. In that sense, he was content with his professional career. At the same time, he was dissatisfied, realizing he hadn't finished what he had started. That fact drove him to strive for more.

Joe Namath illustrates the truth of this Habitude. You've heard this question before: Which is it? Is the tank half-full or half-empty? The answer, of course, depends on whether you are emptying the tank or filling the tank. If you're only using up the fuel, it's half-empty and on its way down. If you are filling it, you see things completely differently. Either way you look at it, however, the tank is only half-full. It serves as a reminder that we must balance two emotions every day: *contentment* and *dissatisfaction*.

We must experience an inward peace, contentment with who we are, and an ability to celebrate what's been accomplished so far. At the same time, we must always maintain a hunger to improve, to grow and become better. In Joe's case, he wanted to become a lifelong learner. I have noticed that depending on our temperament, we tend to manage one half of this equation more naturally than the other. Which one do you have to be more intentional about:

1. Being content with what you have and who you are?

2. Being dissatisfied with what you've achieved, and striving to grow?

When we see things as half-empty, we are often discontented people. We feel we have sacrificed, spending our time and energy without receiving a return on our investment. Often, we compare ourselves to others and feel we've gotten behind. They got all the breaks. *Discontentment* can grind at us internally and wear us down. *Dissatisfaction* is different. We can experience it simultaneously with contentment. We can take pride in our past but still strive for more. When we are dissatisfied, we actually see the tank as half-full, since we are laboring to fill it some more.

On the surface, this appears negative. Outsiders may view you as an unhappy person, as if you feel you haven't received enough. Since you want more, you must be a greedy and maladjusted pessimist, focusing on what you lack. Research proves, however, that there are times when a pessimistic outlook is beneficial. For example, driving in thick fog is a good time to acknowledge that another car may be coming toward you from ahead.

Several studies showed that pessimists were more accurate in their assessments than optimists. In one test, researchers asked people to turn a light switch on and off. The team had actually created a system where the switch had nothing to do with whether the light went on or off. Even when the optimists had no control over the light, though, they actually thought they did. In contrast, the pessimists accurately gauged how much control they had with the light switch. Teams actually benefit from team members who may seem a bit pessimistic. They frequently have a better handle on reality than the optimists.

On the other hand, being optimistic lets us pursue our goals in a positive manner. According to research, optimists tend to respond to positive feedback better[23] and stick to their goals longer. They tend to believe they will figure out a way to win in the end. When optimists are placed in a room with pessimists, these two groups may end up driving each other crazy.[24]

I actually believe we need a little of both. Optimism keeps us happy; pessimism keeps us hungry. Positivity keeps us ready for the future; negativity keeps us rational about the present. When we see the tank with contentment, we anticipate more to come; when we see it with dissatisfaction, we are authentic about the possibilities. We must be both hopeful and honest about our potential. In their book *How Full is Your Bucket,* Tom Rath and Donald Clifton report the following:

1. Nine out of ten people say they are more productive around positive people.

2. Most require some negativity, however, to force them to reflect on their productivity.

3. The average person experiences approximately 20,000 individual moments a day.

4. With too many negative interactions, people want to quit the team or change jobs.

5. More than thirteen positive interactions for every negative one could decrease productivity.

6. The magic ratio: five positive interactions for every one negative interaction.

7. We need to stay both happy and hungry.[25]

I met Liz Murray in 2009. She was already a celebrity, known as the girl who went from "Homeless to Harvard." Liz grew up on the streets of New York City. She loved her parents, but they were both crack addicts and unable to care for her and her sister. Both her mom and dad ended up dying when she was still young, and Liz found herself living on the streets with other homeless kids. All of this could have created a spirit of hopelessness or complacency in Liz. She could have settled for a welfare check every month as she entered adulthood.

But she didn't.

Seeing her life going nowhere, Liz grew very dissatisfied. She visited with a counselor at the one high school that would accept her—and asked what it would take to graduate. This counselor wasn't easy on her—he was gut-level honest. It would be hard, given her track record of absences and lack of test scores as a teen. But he was also a man of faith. He told Liz he would stand with her and support her if she'd give it everything she had.

And she did.

Liz ended up graduating high school. During her senior year, one of her teachers took a few of his promising students to Harvard University—just to see an Ivy League school. While there, Liz caught the "bug" for going to college. She entered a writing contest sponsored by the New York Times—and won. The prize? A scholarship to Harvard University. She graduated years later, and soon she enrolled in graduate school.

Liz Murray is one of the most happy, grateful people I know. She harbors no bitterness about her past. She would say her tank is half-full. At the same time, Liz refused to settle for a life of complacency. She didn't want to just get by. She wanted more, feeling her tank was also half-empty. Somehow, she has balanced the two and done quite well along the way.

In 2005, Steve Jobs gave the commencement speech at Stanford University. In that speech, he echoed this sentiment: "You've got to find what you love….Your work is going to fill a large part of your life, and the only way to be truly satisfied is to do what you believe is great work. And the only way to do great work is to love what you do. If you haven't found it yet, keep looking. Don't settle. As with all matters of the heart, you'll know when you find it. And, like any great relationship, it just gets better and better as the years roll on. So keep looking until you find it. Don't settle."[26]

Talk It Over

1. How are you wired? Are you naturally content or dissatisfied with life?

2. Where do you see this truth in your world? Do you know people who are too much of either?

3. How do you balance dissatisfaction with contentment in your life?

Assess Yourself

As you consider your "tank," remember that you'll need to fill five of them to live a balanced life:

1. Intellectual – You must feed your mind. How are you filling this tank?

2. Physical – You must condition your body. How are you filling this tank?

3. Emotional – You must replenish your heart. How are you filling this tank?

4. Social – You must cultivate adequate friendships. How are you filling this tank?

5. Spiritual – You must feed your soul and your faith. How are you filling this tank?

Try It Out

Reflect for a moment on two situations in your life—one where you are very content and one where you are very dissatisfied. Write down both situations. Try to identify extremes if you can: one where you are perhaps too content (and need to be pushed a little), and one where you may be too dissatisfied (and need to relax a little). Then write a paragraph under each where you describe what a balanced perspective might look like. Finally, jot down an action plan to help you balance being "happy" and "hungry" at the same time.

IMAGE TEN

[Travel Agents
& Tour Guides]

Travel Agents or Tour Guides

THE BIG DIFFERENCE BETWEEN A TRAVEL AGENT AND A TOUR GUIDE IS THIS: ONE GOES WITH YOU AND ONE ONLY TELLS YOU WHERE TO GO. DURING THIS SEASON OF TRANSITION, YOU WILL HAVE MANY TRAVEL AGENTS. YOU MUST FIND A TOUR GUIDE FOR DIRECTION AND SUPPORT.

My wife and I took a vacation to Hawaii with another couple years ago. The trip had been planned perfectly by Janet, our travel agent. Janet knew the islands well and suggested the perfect hotels, points of interest, restaurants and beaches to experience. She gave us brochures to read, maps to study, and choices to make on what tours we wanted to take during our week in Hawaii. It ended up being an incredibly memorable holiday with our friends.

One of the bus tours we chose while in Hawaii required a tour guide to take us to the top of a mountain to see some beautiful waterfalls. His name was Gary. I remember this tour because our guide was a "wanna-be" nightclub comic. No joke. From the moment he stepped onto the bus, Gary was cracking jokes, asking riddles, making puns…trying to make us all laugh. At first, he was amusing, but eventually it got old. We were missing interesting aspects of the tour because Gary was caught up in his jokes. We hated to interrupt him, but ultimately, someone on the bus did. An elderly man spoke up, saying, "Hey, Gary, we appreciate your sense of humor, but we paid money to have an expert take us on a tour, not to hear a stand-up comedian."

We all laughed nervously, and the tour guide got the point. Gary became very helpful the rest of the tour, never missing a chance to show us the points of interest on the tour.

In the end, we were pleased with both our travel agent and our tour guide—but we had very different expectations of both. Janet was only expected to tell us about the trip, to explain where we should go, and then to leave it all up to us once we got there. Gary, on the other hand, was a different story. Tour guides don't merely tell you where to go—they go with you. Tour guides are on the journey right next to you, experiencing every sight and sound along the way. We had a much higher expectation of the tour guide.

This is a picture of life. You will notice as you grow that you'll meet people who will act as "travel agents" and people who will act as "tour guides." Most people find it easier to be a travel agent. In fact, you'll likely have loads of people who will give you advice…and then say, "Good luck with that." Tons of teachers, friends, coaches, employers and counselors will offer their opinion but not get very involved in the journey. It's less expensive for them that way. That's why it's important for you to find a handful of people who are willing to be tour guides—people who not only have wisdom and experience, but who are willing to walk with you through part of your life.

You will likely have many Janets for every one Gary.

During this season of transition, you would be wise to identify a person (or handful of people) who would be willing to play the role of a tour guide. You are making big decisions, connecting with new people, being introduced to new situations and experiences, and embracing a new lifestyle. In these times it's *nice* to have a travel agent—but it's *incredible* to have a tour guide alongside you.

These people can be friends, but often you'll see them as mentors. They are a step ahead of you and are willing to reach back and show the way. They help you maintain perspective and weigh out options. Mentors can be priceless. Years ago, the *Harvard Business Review* published a cover article called "Everyone Who Makes It Has a Mentor." A journalist had interviewed hundreds of successful CEOs to find what they all had in common. What was the key to their wealth and success? The journalist heard a variety of stories—the leaders were both male and female, young and old, single and married. In fact, in the end, they had just one element in common: Every one of them had a mentor.[27] They all had a "tour guide," someone they felt they could call in the middle of the night, if need be—someone they could ask for help, support and counsel.

Is it any wonder that half of the Nobel Peace Prize winners around the world were mentored by previous Peace Prize recipients? Or that many of the most brilliant and talented athletes have a personal trainer? Or that so many business leaders actually invite and pay someone to be an executive coach or life coach for them? This isn't a coincidence. Travel agents are a dime a dozen. Tour guides are almost priceless.

In an earlier chapter we discussed guardrails—which represent standards we set and friends we invite next to us to keep us on track. Tour guides represent one step further: You invite a guide to show you the way, to answer questions, and to help you plan well. The tour guide shows you the right path; the guardrails keep you on that path so you can finish well.

Finishing Well

I will never forget the Summer Olympic Games in 1992. British sprinter Derek Redmond competed in the 400-meter race as a "miracle boy." He had endured many surgeries on his Achilles tendon prior to the race—and yet, he qualified.

But during the competition, tragedy struck again: Derek tore a hamstring, and he tumbled to the ground. Almost as fast as the race had started, it was over. But in classic British style, Derek didn't want to end his career on the ground. So he hoisted himself back up and began hobbling toward the finish line, his face grimacing in pain with each step. I recall saying to my friend as we watched it on TV, "He won't be able to finish this thing alone."

Thank God, he didn't have to. Seated near the top of the stadium that day was Jim, Derek's dad and mentor. He had done everything to prepare Derek to run that race and now could not imagine sitting passively as his mentee limped toward the finish line. He pushed his way past the crowd, jumped over the fence, and began running toward Derek. When he got close enough, Jim put his hand on Derek's shoulder. It must have been a familiar touch, because Derek went a few more paces, then turned and fell into the chest of his mentor. The two just held each other for a moment, as if no one was watching. Jim asked Derek if he was sure he wanted to finish the race. When Derek nodded, Jim placed his arm around Derek and spoke some classic mentor words: "Derek, we started this thing together. Now we are going to finish this thing together."

And that's exactly what they did.[28] In doing so, they furnished us with a vivid picture of a mentor: one who enables another to finish their race well. The Federal Mentoring Council shares that one study of the Big Brothers Big Sisters program found students with mentors earning higher grades than similar students without mentors. A 2007 study discovered that kids in a mentoring relationship at school did better work in class, finished more assigned work, and improved overall in academics—especially in science and in written and oral communication.[29] After graduation, "employees who have had mentors typically earn thousands more than employees who haven't."[30]

What a Mentor Can Help You Do

The following are six issues mentors and mentees can talk about when meeting:

1. Discover your strengths – Identify those natural areas where you add great value.

2. Develop your character – Build qualities, like integrity and discipline, that you'll need in life.

3. Determine your focus – Help you narrow down your interests and pursue the very best.

4. Discern your blind spots – Uncover areas you're unaware of that could sabotage you.

5. Deliver key insights – Reveal the wisdom you'll need as you pursue your goals.

6. Diminish the gap between your potential and your performance.

Author John Crosby once said, "A mentor is a brain to pick, a shoulder to cry on and a kick in the seat of the pants." I say that's something we all need.

Talk It Over

1. What is so valuable about a person in your life who has "been there and done that"?

2. Why is it that "tour guides" are so rare?

3. In what situation could you most use a "tour guide" right now?

4. From the list above (What a Mentor Can Help You Do), which issues do you value most?

Assess Yourself

Examine the list below and evaluate where you most need a "tour guide" in your life:

Issue	Don't need one								Really need one	
1. My academic work:	1	2	3	4	5	6	7	8	9	10
2. To help me spot my strengths and gifts:	1	2	3	4	5	6	7	8	9	10
3. In my relationships: social life and family:	1	2	3	4	5	6	7	8	9	10
4. To help me plan my career goals:	1	2	3	4	5	6	7	8	9	10
5. To enable me to see my blind spots:	1	2	3	4	5	6	7	8	9	10

Try It Out

Carefully reflect on your greatest needs right now—maybe some we listed earlier—your schoolwork, your personal growth, your career planning, your social life, your finances, etc. List the five most relevant needs in your life.

Now begin a list of people who could be mentors for you in those areas. If you list five needs, you may choose up to five different people to "guide" you as you make decisions in those areas. If you don't believe you know anyone who could fill those roles, broaden your scope. Perhaps they're people who live out of town—but you could connect with them by a regular phone call. Maybe they are people on campus you just haven't met yet—a friend could introduce you. In any case, keep in mind that a mentor may look different than you first suspect. Be open. Once you find individuals for your different needs, take them out to coffee or call them, and ask if they'd meet with you so you could ask them some questions. If the meeting goes well, see if they would meet with you on a regular basis, maybe weekly or monthly. This could be the beginning of a great journey.

Backseat Drivers

NO DRIVER ENJOYS SOMEONE IN THE BACKSEAT SCREAMING AT THEM WHERE TO TURN NEXT. SIMILARLY, WE MUST RECOGNIZE WHERE WE ARE SEATED IN RELATIONSHIP TO OTHERS. WE MUST NOT SEEK CONTROL—BUT, WHEN BEHIND THE WHEEL, WE MUST ASSUME RESPONSIBILITY.

My uncle Gene and aunt Wanda are quite a pair. They're both in their eighties now but are still going strong. Both have a sharp mind and a strong will…which has led to some entertaining interactions between the two.

I remember riding in the car with them as a teen. My uncle would drive and my aunt would sit beside him in the passenger seat—but sometimes the roles got reversed. My aunt would furnish ongoing advice and instruction to my uncle on how to drive. As you might guess, he didn't always appreciate the advice. On one ride, after she offered several imperatives, my uncle looked at us in the backseat, smiled, and said, "Sometimes, I get to drive this car all by myself!"

The fact is, most people don't really appreciate "backseat drivers." You know what I'm talking about, don't you? It's the people who aren't behind the wheel but consider themselves driving experts or the human equivalents of a GPS. They're all too happy to tell you how to drive or where to turn next. The dictionary defines a "backseat driver" as 1) a passenger who constantly advises, corrects or nags the driver of a motor vehicle and 2) a meddler who insists on giving unwanted advice. There are two basic problems with backseat drivers:

1. They offer opinions that the person driving has not requested.

2. They confuse their position, assuming the role of the one behind the wheel.

These people are not limited to automobiles.

You can find them everywhere, even on a school campus. They might be students who forget they aren't in a position of authority and make all kinds of demands of others as if they were. It's almost like they are control freaks. They want to *tell* rather than *ask*. While they may mean well, they communicate disrespect or distrust to others. For the driver, "It's like you're playing solitaire and someone starts telling you what cards to put down," says social psychologist Jerry Burger. These people don't value the person who is actually "behind the wheel." They are virtual backseat drivers in life—always acting like the ones in charge.

Now, backseat drivers may actually be offering suggestions because they're afraid, explains Ryan Howes, a psychologist. They can't influence what happens and are scared—what if the driver makes a costly mistake that puts them in danger? Their fear may be explained by their background. "If you grew up in an environment that was kind of chaotic, it's almost a defensive sort of reaction," Burger says. "We've seen this in homes where a parent has an alcohol problem, for example—those children develop a need for control themselves."

In a study Burger led, people were asked for a sample of their blood. The variable was—they could let someone with experience take the sample…or they could do it themselves. Participants "who fit the backseat driver profile—those with a high need for personal control" opted to do it themselves. "Even in that situation, they say, 'Nah, I'll do it myself.' They just can't give that up, even if it means hurting themselves." Psychologist Steven Reiss says, "The backseat driver is an individual who has a strong need to feel influence, and they're always looking for ways to express that need."[31]

This was Aaron's case. As a freshman, he encountered problems in the registrar's office. He had decided to set an appointment and talk over a tuition payment that was late. So far, so good. But when a staff person explained the system and why he'd gotten the notice, the conversation reached an impasse. Aaron felt he had to seize control. He began writing nasty emails, refusing to respond to notices, badgering administrators, and tweeting how horrible his school was. It got worse when he got his parents involved. It wasn't until then that he realized why his emotions had gotten the best of him: His parents had always modeled "control." Whenever things had been challenging, Mom or Dad had always stepped in and taken control. Now…he was following the same pattern.

Learn to TAME Yourself

The fact is, many of us confuse what we have control of and what we don't. It's frustrating and futile to try to manipulate the things that are out of our control. So, what must we do? We must TAME ourselves in four fundamental areas of our lives, taking the wheel in our hands. These are the areas we're responsible for; for all others, we must trust the process:

T – Time.
You choose the way you'll handle your discretionary time. Boss your calendar, and stop letting distractions trip you up. The issue is not prioritizing your schedule, but scheduling your priorities. Take control of your most precious commodity—your calendar.

A – Attitude.
We discussed this in the chapter called "Air Conditioning." Your attitude will make you or break you when it comes to success in school or in a career. Choose your perspective. Don't let others dictate your happiness or the way you see yourself.

M – Money.
Society has set a horrible example for you in managing money. Take control of your spending, saving and giving. Don't let others push you into deeper debt. Make the sacrifices you need to make; don't buy everything you want. As Dave Ramsey says, "Act your wage."

E – Energy.
You decide where to invest your personal energy. The way you use your talent each day is a statement on what you believe is most important. Outside of what your courses, instructors and bosses tell you, you control the rest. Conduct yourself wisely.

On January 13, 2012, the cruise ship *Costa Concordia* hit a rock near Giglio, an island off Italy's Tuscan coast. Hours later, the ship capsized. Fortunately, most of the passengers and crew were able to abandon ship under the chaotic circumstances. Sadly, 32 passengers and crew perished in the tragedy. Costa Cruises indicated later that the ship's captain had sailed off course.

The drama made world news. Captain Francesco Schettino was accused of having left the ship while hundreds of others were still on board. His excuse? He said, "I tripped and I ended up in one of the [life]boats." In contrast, the Coast Guard's Captain Gregorio Maria De Falco had implored Captain Schettino to return and take control of the ship's evacuation. Their heated exchange became a picture of the clash between "hero and antihero," between responsibility and irresponsibility. One Italian journalist said the two captains had "contrasted the 'two souls of Italy'—one represented by a 'cowardly fellow who [fled] his own responsibilities, both as a man and as an official'" and the other by a man who tried to do what was right and responsible. Captain De Falco was quoted as saying, "I am not a hero or an iron man. My team and I just did our duty."[32]

I believe this story provides not only a picture of the "two souls of Italy," but also of the "two souls of mankind." Every one of us is capable of heroic efforts…and complete self-absorption. The key is to understand your role and position. If you aren't in charge, always pause and ask these questions: Do I really need to step in and take charge? Can I relax? Am I able to show respect to the staff and faculty who are in positions of authority? Conversely, if I am responsible for something can I take initiative and act?

Talk It Over

1. Have you observed any "backseat drivers" in your past? How did they make everyone feel?

2. Do you respect your leaders? Do other students respect them? Do you *show* respect to them?

3. Which is hardest for you to be responsible for: your Time, Attitude, Money or Energy?

Assess Yourself

Read the statements below. Indicate whether it is easy, normal or hard for you to practice the attitudes in the statements. Then discuss your answers:

1. I show consistent respect for my leaders.	Easy	Normal	Hard
2. I trust my leaders, even when I disagree.	Easy	Normal	Hard
3. I can submit to them even when I don't understand.	Easy	Normal	Hard
4. I don't have to be "in control" to enjoy my day.	Easy	Normal	Hard

Try It Out

This week, look for two situations where you can practice the principle in this chapter:

1. Find a situation where you're tempted to be a "backseat driver" and to seize control.

2. Find a situation where you must be responsible but are tempted to look to someone else.

Consider your appropriate role. If someone else is in charge, how hard is it for you to trust them? What are you tempted to do instead of trust? What must you do to stay *under control* instead of *in control,* and simply go with the flow? If you are the one who needs to take initiative and act, how hard is it to "take the wheel"? Are you tempted to play the victim in this situation and blame someone else when something goes wrong? What do you need to do to take responsibility?

IMAGE TWELVE

[Shortcut or
Second Mile]

Shortcut or Second Mile

IN LIFE, WE ARE CONDITIONED TO LOOK FOR SHORTCUTS. WE SEEK THE MOST COMFORTABLE AND EASY AND FAMILIAR WAY TO GET BY. THOSE WHO GO THE EXTRA MILE MAY WORK HARDER, BUT THEY REAP BENEFITS THROUGH THEIR SERVICE THAT NO ONE ELSE EXPERIENCES.

You and I grew up in a culture and society where we were conditioned to look for shortcuts. Whatever gets you what you want the fastest—take it. We don't want to read the whole book, just the CliffsNotes. We don't have time for the conventional oven, so we use the microwave. We wish for time to eat a full breakfast—but we can only handle an instant breakfast. And as for research…well, we have a "Google reflex." Let's be honest—we know better, but our world has taught us to simply take the straightest line to the goal.

Do you remember the story of the Tortoise and the Hare? It's a classic children's story we all heard growing up, about a race between a rabbit and a turtle. Everyone places bets on the rabbit to win—after all, he is a fast, nimble creature. The turtle, on the other hand—bless his heart—is as slow as a creature can get. He plods along at a…well, at a turtle's pace.

But the story has a moral to it. Do you remember?

In the end, the rabbit gets so far ahead of the turtle, he gets a little cocky. In his arrogance, he wanders off the path and decides to take a nap. While he is sleeping for hours, the turtle not only catches up with him but actually finishes first. The plodder beats the pacesetter. Hmmm. Sounds familiar.

When I use my GPS on the road, I almost always choose the "fastest route" option. Not the scenic route, not the alternative route, but the one that gets me to my destination most quickly. In fact, I love shortcuts. One time, I remember getting lost because I was so determined to find a shortcut to my goal. I got so preoccupied with speed, I got lost. I was so frustrated about not wasting time, I lost more time. My worry blinded me from seeing what to do next. The "fastest" path ended up taking me longer than any of the others. This is often a picture of life.

There's nothing wrong with efficiency. I love to work smart, not just hard. But when I get lost within speed, convenience and efficiency, I frequently lose sight of what gives my life meaning—the people around me I love; the scenery I could enjoy if I slowed down; offering something to this world that could improve it. There are some places we can't reach by a shortcut.

Derek and Rachel have similar stories. They went to different colleges, but they were both doing horribly their freshman year. Their grades had tanked, they missed their families, and relationships with fellow students on campus just weren't jelling. While Derek got "stuck" in his dilemma, Rachel decided to attack her challenge head-on by looking beyond her problems and getting her mind off herself. She gave blood and recruited others to do so as well. She also began working at National Student Partnerships, an organization founded at Yale to help people in the local community with whatever they needed, including finding jobs. Ironically, it was when Rachel got her mind on others that her problems began to evaporate. They all but took care of themselves. However, Derek became depressed with his situation and quit school. He couldn't get beyond himself.

The Second Mile

Derek and Rachel were not obligated to help anyone. Rachel's sacrificial service to others, however, was a "bonus" that served her well; in fact, it may have saved her college career. You might say she went "the second mile." This term actually comes from the ancient Roman Empire. Centuries ago, when Rome controlled many countries as colonies, citizens in those countries were obligated to help soldiers if they requested it. Roman military could ask people to carry their equipment for them, for up to a mile. It was a law most citizens resented. For some, however, it was an opportunity to win over the soldiers. When the mile was finished, the soldiers expected to retrieve their equipment and continue on their own, or impose it on someone else. Those citizens who understood this "second mile" principle, however, would refuse to set it down—they'd offer to carry it a second mile. I can imagine the conversations that occurred during that extra mile. I'm sure the soldiers asked them why they were doing more than expected. Perhaps they'd ask about their lives or families. It must have felt different—the citizens weren't serving out of obligation, but because they wanted to. Let me break down the differences between the first and second miles:

First Mile	Second Mile
You walk it because you have to.	You walk it because you want to.
Doing the minimum.	Doing the maximum.
It's about duty.	It's about devotion.
Satisfies necessities.	Serves needs.
Focus is on me.	Focus is on others.

As you can tell, "second mile" living is about service. It requires you to focus on others, not on your own survival. We tend to admire people who live this way. Decades ago, Mahatma Gandhi was boarding a train with a number of companions. One of his shoes fell off and disappeared in the gap between the train and the platform. Unable to retrieve it, he took off his other shoe and threw it down beside the first.

When his fellow travelers asked why he had done that, Gandhi explained that a person who finds one shoe is not better off—what's helpful is finding a pair. Gandhi was a second-mile guy.

Why It's Hard For Us Today

Sometimes when we give our time, money and energy, we save ourselves from our self-absorbed ways. Consider for a moment the SCENE that students are growing up in today:

Our Culture Values...	So We Tend to Think...
S – Speed	Slow is bad.
C – Convenience	Hard is bad.
E – Entertainment	Boring is bad.
N – Nurture	Risk is bad.
E – Entitlement	Labor is bad.

The problem is—by avoiding the items in the right column above, we avoid the very elements that enable us to mature and get beyond our own selfish lifestyle. Both students and adults can be downright narcissistic. This makes for an unhappy life. Someone once said, "The smallest packages in the world are people who are wrapped up in themselves."

Data from the US Department of Education furnishes us with a remedy. A National Education Longitudinal Study demonstrates that students who get involved in community service stay more engaged in school.[33] In fact, they may develop a clearer vision for life after graduation. In other words, when students begin to give their lives away—whether it's donating blood to the Red Cross, or tutoring a troubled middle school kid, or painting and cleaning up poor neighborhoods—they actually help themselves. When we give, we always receive.

The story is told of a group of rock climbers touring through some snowy mountains in Asia. It became stormy and was so bitterly cold that one of the young men fainted in the snow. Several from the group said that they felt bad but they couldn't do anything to save their friend. If they didn't continue, they would all freeze to death. One climber, however, couldn't do that. He told the others to go ahead; he would not leave his friend lying in the snow to die.

The others proceeded quickly into the storm while this lone man picked up his unconscious friend and carried him over the mountain. Several hours later, the man carrying his friend came upon the others lying in the snow. They had all frozen from the icy temperatures. He, however, was still warm from carrying his friend on his shoulders. Giving his life to save someone else…had actually saved his own life.

I'd call that second-mile living.

Talk It Over

1. Why do you think it's so easy in our culture to become self-absorbed?

2. What are the areas where you are prone to get "lost" in your own problems?

3. Talk about a time when you chose to get involved in helping someone else. How did you feel?

Assess Yourself

Assess yourself on each continuum below. Be honest as you place an X in the appropriate spot. When finished, discuss how you answered. How could you improve?

a. When I encounter a problem, I tend to:

|--|
focus on the problem only by myself   include others in solving the problem

b. Left to myself, I am naturally a:

|--|
shortcut person   second-mile person

c. When I am with a group of people, I tend to:

|--|
become self-conscious and withdraw   look outward and see how i can help others

Try It Out

This one is easy. As soon as you can, find a place to serve. If possible, serve some people you don't know well and who cannot do anything for you in return. Focus completely on giving your time and energy generously to others. This can take place on your school campus, at your work, or in your local community. If possible, make this a regular practice. In the past, students have served at hospitals, retirement homes and hospices, prisons, soup kitchens—you name it. Once you finish, ask this question: Who benefited more—the people you served, or you? Talk it over.

IMAGE THIRTEEN [The Destinat vs. th

The Destination vs. the Trip

PEOPLE CAN BE DIVIDED INTO TWO GROUPS: THOSE WHO ARE IN IT ONLY TO REACH A GOAL, AND THOSE WHO JUST ENJOY THE JOURNEY. ACTUALLY, BOTH ATTITUDES ARE GOOD. ONCE YOU CHOOSE THE RIGHT DESTINATION, THE JOURNEY CAN BECOME PART OF THE SATISFACTION.

If you drive on any road today, you'll see a Honda somewhere. The Honda auto company has become a well-respected enterprise worldwide. I appreciate them all the more because I know the story behind how this company got started.

Early on, Soichiro Honda developed a piston ring and tried to sell it to Toyota Motor Corporation. He had to endure being rejected and keep improving the piston ring until Toyota finally gave him a contract. Unfortunately, Japan was preparing for war at the time, and problems arose in funding the factory Honda needed. The idea could have died. Instead of quitting, though, Honda switched his strategy and developed a formula to make his own concrete so he could build a factory.[34]

During the war, however, his factory was leveled by a bomb. Again, Honda didn't quit. He gathered fuel cans discarded by air fighters, which let him continue manufacturing (he called the fuel cans "gifts from President Truman"[35]). Moving forward once again, Honda was finally on his way to productivity. Then…an earthquake destroyed his factory, forcing him to sell his operation to Toyota.

After the earthquake, Honda was at a fork in the road: to quit or to try again. He chose to try again. Now, there was a major gas shortage after the war. When Mr. Honda couldn't afford to drive his car, he attached a small motor to his bicycle, cutting his fuel costs by 80%. This was a breakthrough, and people around him started wanting bikes like this. When Honda ran out of motors to attach to their bikes, he decided to build another factory—this time to make motors. He sent a letter to all 18,000 bicycle shops in Japan and got enough capital from them to start the factory. After it was built, Honda continued to improve his "motorized bike," and soon…the successful Honda motorcycle was born.[36] He later exported his invention to Europe and the US, and followed up with many cars afterward. Today, the Honda corporation employs 180,000 people and is one of the largest automobile manufacturers in Japan and in the world.

I love this story because it illustrates a final principle for us as we navigate transitions. I call it The Destination vs. the Trip. Have you ever noticed that some people are really into their goals, while others are only into living from day to day, just enjoying the journey? I believe both lifestyles are important, but it's difficult to balance the two. Mr. Honda believed in his journey and somehow found satisfaction in conquering his day-to-day challenges. I believe he could do this because he was so convinced that his goal was worthwhile. All the setbacks, hurdles and barriers did not deter him from his goal. The stumbling blocks became the stepping stones. The obstacles became opportunities. The problems became possibilities. Someone once said, "Successful people build their dreams from the bricks others throw at them."

Mr. Honda believed in his journey and could endure because he was sure of his destination. This conviction enabled him to keep finding ways to make progress. May I ask you a question?

Do you have a great goal?

Choosing the right destination for yourself makes a world of difference in whether you will enjoy the daily grind. Roads can have potholes, curves, rocks and traffic jams. If you're looking forward to your destination, all those hardships are worth it.

What's Your Destination?

If you've yet to establish a big-picture goal for your life, try responding to these questions:

1. What are your talents, strengths and skills? Are you gifted to do anything?

2. What are your passions? What do you love doing that could become a career?

3. What are your "burdens"? Do any big problems in the world upset and motivate you?

4. What are your dreams? What do you imagine doing with your life?

5. What are your values? Do you have a set of values that guide your choices?

6. What are your results? What is it you do that really produces results?

7. What is your affirmation? What do others recognize in you as a unique trait?

8. What are your themes? Do you have topics you find yourself talking about a lot?

9. What is your fulfillment? What do you do that feels deeply rewarding inside?

10. What are your experiences? Have you had hallmark experiences that may be valuable?

11. What are your prospects? Are there any opportunities in front of you now?

Once you choose a destination, commit to it. Sure—it may change along the way, but the only way you'll know if a goal is right is to sink your teeth into it and really give it your all. The Scottish mountaineer W. H. Murray wrote, "Until one is committed, there is hesitancy, the chance to draw back, always ineffectiveness. Concerning all acts of initiative (and creation), there is one elementary truth the ignorance of which kills countless ideas and splendid plans: that the moment one definitely commits oneself, then providence moves too. All sorts of things occur to help one that would never otherwise have occurred. A whole stream of events issues from the decision, raising in one's favor all manner of unforeseen incidents, meetings and material assistance, which no man could have dreamt would have come his way....Whatever you can do or dream you can, begin it. Boldness has genius, power and magic in it!"[37]

Goal Setting Tips

For years, business leaders have taught that successful people set SMART goals:

S – Specific (Make your goals clear and precise, not fuzzy and vague.)

M – Measurable (Make goals tangible enough that they can be measured.)

A – Attainable (Set realistic goals—not so big they seem impossible.)

R – Relevant (Set goals that stretch you yet match your identity.)

T – Timely (Make goals fit into the time frame you can manage.)

Burn Your Boats

If you've set SMART goals, you have a much better chance at enjoying the journey, day by day. In fact, each day becomes another step toward your destination and becomes rewarding. Let me be clear: The single greatest factor impacting whether you enjoy your "trip" is—*committing to it*.

The ancient Greek warriors were both feared and respected by their enemies. In battle, the Greeks established a well-deserved reputation for their unsurpassed bravery and unshakable commitment to victory. The key to their overwhelming success on the battlefield had far more to do with how the Greek commanders motivated the warriors than it did with issues of tactics or training. The Greeks were master motivators who understood how to use a "dramatic demonstration" to infuse a spirit of commitment into the heart of every warrior. Once the warriors had been offloaded from their boats onto their enemy's shore, the Greek commanders would shout out their first order:

"Burn the boats!"

The sight of burning boats removed any notion of retreat from their hearts and any thoughts of surrender from their heads. Imagine the tremendous psychological impact on the soldiers as they watched their boats being torched. As the boats slipped quietly out of sight into the water, each man understood there was no turning back and the only way home was through victory.

Legendary football coach Vince Lombardi said, "The quality of a person's life is in direct proportion to their commitment to excellence, regardless of their chosen field of endeavor."[38]

Talk It Over

1. What are the advantages of an attitude that merely enjoys the journey day by day?

2. What are the advantages of an attitude that envisions a goal and pursues that target?

3. Which attitude do you tend to have? Do you balance these two perspectives well?

Assess Yourself

Evaluate your responses to the statements below. A low score means you can't agree with the statement. A high score means you definitely practice it. Discuss your answers:

1. I have set specific and meaningful goals for myself.

   1 2 3 4 5 6 7 8 9 10

2. These goals motivate me each day.

   1 2 3 4 5 6 7 8 9 10

3. My goals help me enjoy the journey day by day.

   1 2 3 4 5 6 7 8 9 10

4. I am absolutely committed to reaching my goals.

   1 2 3 4 5 6 7 8 9 10

5. I find fulfillment in making progress toward my goals.

   1 2 3 4 5 6 7 8 9 10

Try It Out

This week, take some time to jot down your responses to the questions in this chapter:

1. What are your talents, strengths and skills? Are you gifted to do anything?

2. What are your passions? What do you love doing that could become a career?

3. What are your "burdens"? Do any big problems in the world upset and motivate you?

4. What are your dreams? What do you imagine doing with your life?

5. What are your values? Do you have a set of values that guide your choices?

6. What are your results? What is it you do that really produces results?

7. What is your affirmation? What do others recognize in you as a unique trait?

8. What are your themes? Do you have topics you find yourself talking about a lot?

9. What is your fulfillment? What do you do that feels deeply rewarding inside?

10. What are your experiences? Have you had hallmark experiences that may be valuable?

11. What are your prospects? Are there any opportunities in front of you now?

Do your responses have any common threads? When you see those common threads, set some SMART goals. Connect the big picture to the day-to-day grind. Then…enjoy the journey.

[Reflect and Respond]

Below, jot down your major thoughts, ideas and conclusions from this book...

Acknowledgements

I want to give a shout out to a handful of people who helped create this book. Special thanks to Jake Sumner, Jonathan Elmore and Katlyn Moncrief for their help with research. Also to Brett Wilkes for his help with editing and footnotes. Finally, thanks a million Jeff Gribble for making this book look so good. I loved doing the journey with you.

[End Notes]

1 Josh Linkner, "Grit: The Top Predictor of Success," *Fast Company*, December 12, 2011. http://www.fastcompany.com/1800541/grit-top-predictor-success

2 Roy Disney, quoted in John Greathouse, "Decision Making 101 – Defining Your Values Makes Most Decisions Easy," *Business Insider*, July 29, 2011. http://articles.businessinsider.com/2011-07-29/tech/30033751_1_software-engineer-full-time-decision

3 Luke Meredith, "Joel Northrup Refuses to Face Cassy Herkelman: Iowa Wrestler Won't Face Girl," *The Huffington Post*, February 17, 2011. http://www.huffingtonpost.com/2011/02/17/joel-northup-cassy-herkelman_n_824649.html

4 Po Bronson and Ashley Merryman, *NurtureShock: New Thinking About Children* (New York: Twelve, 2009), 52-53.

5 Daniel S. Levy/Lincoln, Larry Trapp and Michael Weisser, "The Cantor and the Klansman: Weisser, Trapp," *Time*, February 17, 1992. http://www.time.com/time/subscriber/printout/0,8816,974903,00.html

6 Thomas H. Holmes and Richard H. Rahe, "The social readjustment rating scale," *Journal of Psychosomatic Research* 11.2 Aug. (1967): 213-18.

7 Matt McMillen, "To the Brain, Getting Burned, Getting Dumped Feel the Same," *CNN Health*, March 29, 2011. http://www.cnn.com/2011/HEALTH/03/28/burn.heartbreak.same.to.brain/index.html

8 Paul Harvey, "The Eskimo and the Wolf," *The Florence Times*, (Florence, AL), August 21, 1966, 4. http://bit.ly/HarveyIllustration

9 Deirdre van Dyke, "Parlez-Vous Twixters?" *Time*, January 24, 2005, http://www.time.com/time/magazine/article/0,9171,1018084,00.html

10 Jessica Anderson, "Life After College for Many Means Returning Home," *The Baltimore Sun*, June 20, 2010. http://articles.baltimoresun.com/2010-06-20/news/bs-md-recent-grads-living-at-home-20100620_1_job-market-graduate-school-marketing-firm

11 Jack Cafferty, "Is the decline of American schools putting national security at risk?" *CNN*, March 21, 2012. http://caffertyfile.blogs.cnn.com/2012/03/21/is-u-s-education-failure-a-national-security-threat/

12 Laura Sessions Stepp, "Adolescence: Not Just for Kids," *The Washington Post*, January 2, 2002. http://www.washingtonpost.com/ac2/wp-dyn/A49581-2002Jan1?language=printer

13 Victor Goertzel and Mildred George Goertzel, *Cradles of Eminence* (Boston: Little, Brown and Co, 1962).

[14] Donald Miller, "Why Conflict in Life is Terrific, and How to Change Your Attitude About It," *Storyline Blog*, March 28, 2012. http://storylineblog.com/2012/03/28/the-beauty-of-conflict/

[15] Roy F. Baumeister and John Tierney, *Willpower: Rediscovering the Greatest Human Strength* (New York: Penguin Press, 2011), 163.

[16] Eric Greitens, "The SEAL Sensibility," *The Wall Street Journal*, May 7, 2011. http://online.wsj.com/article/SB10001424052748703992704576307021339210488.html

[17] Tonya Hurley, quoted in Kaylee Page, "Expectations are Our Energy Drinks," *Plywood People*, May 10, 2012. http://plywoodpeople.com/10497

[18] Wayne W. Dyer, *Pulling Your Own Strings* (New York: Quill, 2001), 11.

[19] Malcolm Gladwell, *The Tipping Point: How Little Things Can Make a Big Difference* (Boston: Little, Brown, 2000), 180-182.

[20] Catey Hill, "Microsoft Mogul Bill Gates Leaves Facebook Because He Had 'Too Many Friends,'" *New York Daily News*, July 27, 2009. http://articles.nydailynews.com/2009-07-27/news/17928569_1_facebook-microsoft-friends

[21] Alex Williams, "It's Not Me, It's You," *The New York Times*, January 28, 2012. http://www.nytimes.com/2012/01/29/fashion/its-not-me-its-you-how-to-end-a-friendship.html?_r=1&pagewanted=all

[22] Diane Mapes, "Toxic Friends? 8 in 10 People Endure Poisonous Pals," *TODAY*, August 22, 2011. http://today.msnbc.msn.com/id/44205822/ns/today-today_health/t/toxic-friends-people-endure-poisonous-pals/

[23] Donald Miller, "Do You Filter Your Relationships? You Probably Should," *Storyline Blog*, March 26, 2012. http://storylineblog.com/2012/03/26/do-you-filter-your-relationships-you-probably-should/

[24] Henry Cloud, *Necessary Endings* (New York: HarperBusiness, 2010), 202-208.

[25] Emily Jupp, "Are You an Oscar or an Elmo?" *The Independent*, July 31, 2012. http://www.independent.co.uk/life-style/health-and-families/features/are-you-an-oscar-or-an-elmo-7987835.html

[26] James C. Collins, *Good to Great: Why Some Companies Make the Leap—and Others Don't* (New York: HarperBusiness, 2001), 83-88.

[27] Jeremy Dean, "Pessimism vs. Optimism," *Psych Central*, 2011. http://psychcentral.com/blog/archives/2011/03/17/pessimism-vs-optimism/

[28] Shelley Holmes, "Optimism vs. Pessimism." http://www.leadership-and-motivation-training.com/optimism-vs-pessimism.html

[29] Tom Rath and Donald O. Clifton. *How Full Is Your Bucket?* Positive Strategies for Work and Life (New York: Gallup Press, 2004).

[30] Steve Jobs, Stanford University Commencement Speech Prepared Text, June 12, 2005. http://news.stanford.edu/news/2005/june15/jobs-061505.html

[31] Eliza G. C. Collins and Patricia Scott, eds., "Everyone Who Makes It Has a Mentor," *Harvard Business Review*, 56 (no. 4, July-August 1978), 89-101.

[32] Derek Redmond, http://www.derekredmond.com/profile.asp

[33] "What are the Benefits of Mentoring?" Federal Mentoring Council. http://www.federalmentoringcouncil.gov/benefits.asp

[34] American Speech-Language-Hearing Association, "The Benefits of Mentoring." http://www.asha.org/students/gatheringplace/MentBen/

[35] Josh Linkner, "The Dirty Little Secret of Overnight Success," *Fast Company*, April 3, 2012. http://www.fastcompany.com/1826976/dirty-little-secret-overnight-successes

[36] Elizabeth Svoboda, "Field Guide to the Backseat Driver: Pedal to the Meddle," *Psychology Today*, May 19, 2011. http://www.psychologytoday.com/print/44470

[37] Gaia Pianigiani and Alan Cowell, "Captain of Stricken Vessel Says He Fell Overboard in Passenger Panic," *The New York Times*, January 18, 2012. http://www.nytimes.com/2012/01/19/world/europe/costa-concordia-italy-cruise-ship-rescue-suspended.html

[38] "Extracurricular Participation and Student Engagement," National Center for Education Statistics," June 1995. http://nces.ed.gov/pubs95/web/95741.asp

[39] Anthony Robbins, *Notes from a Friend: A Quick and Simple Guide to Taking Charge of Your Life* (New York: Fireside, 1995), 36-39.

[40] Ty Kiisel, "Dana Vollmer: The Definition of What it Really Means to be a Champion," *Forbes*, July 31, 2012. http://www.forbes.com/sites/tykiisel/2012/07/31/dana-vollmer-the-definition-of-what-it-really-means-to-be-a-champion/

[41] Robbins.

[42] W. H. Murray, *The Scottish Himalayan Expedition* (London: Dent, 1951).

[43] Vince Lombardi, "Famous Quotes by Vince Lombardi." http://www.vincelombardi.com/quotes.html

Enjoy Habitudes?

Help us bring these lessons to students who can't afford them.

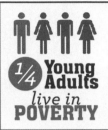

1/4 Young Adults *live in* **POVERTY**

8/10 Young Adults *plan to* **MOVE HOME** *after College*

In both urban and rural environments, **students are sheltered** *within a 9-mile radius of their home,* **shielded from experiences** *that involve risk or failure.* **This leads to delayed maturity.**

All over the country and in developing nations around the world, there are students who are not equipped to lead themselves (or others) into the next steps of their lives. What's worse, their schools can't afford leadership development materials to help them mature into the best versions of themselves.

We want to change that. We want to help students broaden their vision, take bigger risks, think bigger thoughts, and pursue bigger goals.

To do this, we created **The Growing Leaders Initiative**, to provide *Habitudes* in schools and youth non-profit organizations that cannot afford to purchase programs for their students. Thanks to donor support, grants are available for qualified applicants.

To apply or donate, visit
www.**TheGrowingLeadersInitiative**.com.

The
GROWING LEADERS
Initiative